English Garden Cities

An introduction

English Garden Cities

An introduction

Mervyn Miller

ENGLISH HERITAGE

Letchworth Garden City
Heritage Foundation

Front cover
Howard Cottage Society housing, Rushby Mead, Letchworth, 1911, designed by Robert Bennett and Wilson Bidwell, remains the epitome of garden city design values.
[DP088230]

Inside front cover
Rebuilding the 16th-century Selly Manor House at Bournville provided a layer of 'instant history'.
[Mervyn Miller]

Frontispiece
Ebenezer Howard (1850–1928) by Spenser Pryse, presented to him at a Garden Cities and Town Planning Association dinner in March 1912.
[Letchworth Garden City Heritage Foundation]

Acknowledgements
The sweeping vista of Parkway at Welwyn Garden City provides a fitting tribute to Louis de Soissons, its master-planner and architect.
[DP088359]

Inside back cover
Lest we forget: the gravitas and drama of the war memorial at Port Sunlight pays tribute to the fallen defenders of the realm (1916–22, sculptor: William Goscombe John).
[Mervyn Miller]

Back cover
Attractive envelope stickers publicising 'Civic Week', held in Letchworth in 1935.
[Mervyn Miller]

Published by English Heritage, The Engine House, Fire Fly Avenue, Swindon SN2 2EH
www.english-heritage.org.uk
English Heritage is the Government's statutory adviser on all aspects of the historic environment.

© English Heritage 2010

Images (except as otherwise shown) © English Heritage, © Crown Copyright. EH,or Reproduced by permission of English Heritage.

Figs 12, 30, 32, 38, 39, 43, 47, 65, 67, 70 and 73 are now © Garden City Collection, Letchworth Garden City Heritage Foundation.

First published 2010
Reprinted 2015

ISBN 978 1 84802 051 1

Product code 51532

British Library Cataloguing in Publication Data
A CIP catalogue record for this book is available from the British Library.

The National Monuments Record is the public archive of English Heritage. For more information, contact NMR Enquiry and Research Services, National Monuments Record Centre, Kemble Drive, Swindon SN2 2GZ; telephone (01793) 414600.

Typeset in ITC Charter 9.25pt on 13pt

Photographs by Pat Payne
Aerial photographs by Damian Grady and Dave MacLeod
Graphics by Philip Sinton
Brought to publication by Jess Ward, Publishing, English Heritage
Edited by Barry Page
Page layout by Simon Borrough
Printed in Belgium by DeckersSnoeck

Contents

Acknowledgements

This book followed a collaborative study by the Town and Country Planning Association and English Heritage on 'The Future of Garden City Communities', on which I was an advisor, which ran from 2004 to 2008. However, my garden city credentials go back over 35 years, to the dawn of their recording and conservation. It has been a great pleasure to revisit the subject. I should like to thank the following individuals and organisations for their assistance, which has added value to the book, in particular by providing archive illustrations:

Sue Flood, County Archivist, Hertfordshire Archives and Local Studies; Hampstead Garden Suburb Archives Trust; Tracy Harvey, Head of Development Control, Welwyn Hatfield Council; Alan Henderson, Brentham Society Archivist; Alan Howard, Director of Marketing and PR, Letchworth Garden City Heritage Foundation, for support of the publication; John Rylands Library, University of Manchester; Letchworth Museum and Art Gallery; London Metropolitan Archives; Jonathan Makepeace, Assistant Curator, Photograph Collection, Royal Institute of British Architects; Sheila Murray, who typed all the initial drafts and captions; Jane Parr of Manchester Archives and Local Studies; Chris Sedgwick and Mark Ellison of Wythenshawe Regeneration Team; Josh Tidy, Curator of First Garden City Heritage Museum; Sian Woodward, Acting Curator, Letchworth Museum and Art Gallery.

English Heritage has assisted in myriad ways: Colum Giles, Head of Urban Research, gave invaluable advice on editing the text; Pat Payne took many of the photographs, including the cover illustration; Philip Sinton drew the maps; while Damian Grady and David MacLeod produced new aerial photographs bringing out the verdant maturity of the major settlements.

THIS GARDEN IS A MEMORIAL TO LOUIS DE SOISSONS 1890-1962 WHO DESIGNED THIS TOWN

Foreword

By the middle of the 19th century, over half of Britain's population lived in towns: in 1900 the proportion had risen to over three-quarters. Combined with rapid population growth, this represented a transformation in Britain's demography: the modern world had been created. However, English towns and cities presented social and environmental problems of unprecedented scale, and much of Britain's history in this period is connected with efforts to ameliorate the frightening conditions in which large numbers of people lived. Out of these efforts emerged the Garden City Movement, a visionary alternative to the apparent chaos of contemporary towns and perhaps one of England's most radical contributions to urban planning. Better housing, more space and a new relationship between town and country lay at the heart of Ebenezer Howard's efforts to create a new civilisation in a better environment.

This book tells the story of garden cities and garden city settlements. The significance of the movement has sometimes been overlooked. Howard's ideas inspired not just the handful of settlements with the 'garden city' tag, but also housing provision in almost every town in the country as well as further afield. Garden city settlements are, therefore, important: they have special qualities beyond the picturesque, with high standards of design in architecture and landscaping. However, they are fragile environments. Some are over 100 years old. Of course they served a lifestyle very different from that of today. Adaptation to increased pressure for change, both from planning and regeneration, as well as, the numerous small, humdrum interventions consequent upon modern living can tip the balance to the point at which the manifest reasons why garden cities have proved so popular are seriously endangered. This would be in nobody's interests. Garden cities must adapt to survive, but we must seek to find solutions which allow them to evolve while at the same time retaining their character. English Heritage is committed to working with its partners – local authorities, community groups, trusts, developers and so on – so that these unique environments can continue to be enjoyed in the future. Good conservation, informed by a thorough understanding of what makes these places special, is the means by which the competing demands upon garden city settlements can be reconciled: the future depends upon the care with which we treat these places today.

Baroness Andrews, Chair of English Heritage

1

Visions for change: reforming the 19th-century city

Familiarity with the term 'garden city' is not necessarily accompanied by an appreciation of either its meaning or significance. Why pair these words? What is a 'garden city', and what makes it different? Today, more than a century after the first garden city was begun, it is all too easy to forget its original impact and to overlook its influence, and that of its successors, over the design of towns and cities throughout England and beyond. The Garden City Movement transcended design, however, for it originated in environmental and social concerns. The founder of the movement, Ebenezer Howard (1850–1928), called the garden city 'the peaceful path to real reform'; he saw it as the physical setting for a radically different lifestyle, involving a 'joyous union' of town and country, from which 'will spring a new hope, a new life, a new civilisation'.[1]

Industrialisation and urbanisation

The garden city reacted to the failure of the 19th-century industrial city, justly parodied as 'Coketown' by Charles Dickens in *Hard Times*, to address its inherent social and environmental problems. The population of England and Wales rose between 1801 and 1901 from 8.9 to 32.6 million, and that of London from 864,000 to 4.5 million, through hasty, intensive and uncontrolled urbanisation. This brought pollution, cholera and appalling housing conditions, revealed by observers such as Dr James Phillips Kay (1804–77) in Manchester in the 1830s and (Sir) Edwin Chadwick (1801–90) in London in the 1840s. In the 1880s, Charles Booth's (1840–1916) massive *Life and Labour of the People of London* recorded that 35 per cent of east London's population of 900,000 were in the lowest three categories of poverty, inhabiting the worst, ill-maintained and overcrowded housing.

Statistics fascinated the Victorians: mortality, occupancy rates and population density quantified urban problems with precision, yet barely chronicled the human misery. They did, however, stimulate action. Public health legislation, enforced through the granting of wider powers to local authorities, led to slum clearance and statutory controls over drainage and building construction. It was recognised that provision of decent housing for the mass of the urban population was the key to progress and that this might

Port Sunlight displayed a catalogue of styles, including the Arts and Crafts revival of Cheshire timber-framed construction, in this group at the junction of Lower Road and Central Road, 1907, by J Lomax Simpson. [Mervyn Miller]

be achieved without radical change. Organisations such as the Peabody Trust in London demonstrated, through 'five per cent philanthropy', the financial viability of building improved working-class housing. The pioneer of social work, Octavia Hill (1838–1912), undertook housing management. Among her assistants were Beatrice Webb (1858–1943) (née Potter, who with her husband, Sidney Webb (1859–1947), became a leader in municipal Socialism) and Henrietta Barnett (1851–1936) (subsequently founder of Hampstead Garden Suburb). Local authorities became providers of housing in the 1890s, especially the London County Council, whose Millbank scheme in Pimlico (1898–1905) was hailed for innovative standards and robust designs. The broader vision of a Hegelian concept of progress, the Benthamite maxim of the greatest good for the greatest number, Utopian philosophy, Christian and Fabian socialism, the rise of governmental intervention and the Garden City and Arts and Crafts Movements represented a potent mix of idealism and pragmatism, which helped to define community building at the end of the 19th century.

Ebenezer Howard and the garden city: planning visionary or heroic simpleton?

Howard defined the garden city as the alternative to unrestrained urban development and, it should be remembered, the profound depression in rural areas. His friend, the playwright George Bernard Shaw (1856–1950) wrote of Howard as 'one of those heroic simpletons who do big things whilst our prominent worldlings are explaining why they are Utopian and impossible. And of course it is they who will make money out of his work.'[2]

The garden city was Howard's 'big idea' and it gained worldwide acclaim. Shaw, although characteristically sceptical, had supported the development of Letchworth and Welwyn Garden Cities and invested in co-partnership housing. The Fabian Society, of which Shaw was a prominent member, was initially hostile to the garden city, but later became more sympathetic, although favouring public sector delivery.

Born in Fore Street in the City of London, Howard joined Greaves and Son, stockbrokers, at the age of 15. Outwardly conventional but often personally impulsive, he decamped to the United States in 1871. After failing at homestead farming (ironically in Howard County, Nebraska) he retreated to Chicago to work as a law stenographer. He witnessed the emergence of the skyscraper in the 'loop' central business district during rebuilding after the 1871 fire, and saw the spreading residential suburbs west of the city, notably Riverside, planned by Frederick Law Olmsted (1822–1903), famed for Central Park in New York. Returning to England in 1876, Howard became a parliamentary reporter. Transcribing lengthy debates, committees and Government commissions, he noted the unanimity of opinion on the failure of cities to address their social and environmental problems, but was personally concerned by the limitations of governmental intervention. This provoked his well-known scepticism of parliamentary procedure as an agent of long-term reform. In 1879, he married Elizabeth Ann Bills (1854–1904), daughter of a Nuneaton innkeeper. 'Lizzie' was his ideal partner, running the household on slender means and supporting his increasing involvement with social issues, as Howard slowly defined his 'peaceful path to real reform'.

Howard's reading was omnivorous, yet discriminating. The anarchism of Peter Kropotkin (1842–1921), the land reform and single tax promises of Henry George (1839–97), the Utopianism of Thomas More (1478–1535), the evolving socialism of John Ruskin (1819–1900) and William Morris (1834–96), all appealed to him. Prime influences were the theory of organised population migration by Edward Gibbon Wakefield (1796–1862) and Alfred Marshall (1842–1924); the land tenure trust concept of Thomas Spence (1750–1814) and Herbert Spencer (1820–1903), through which increase in value was returned to the community; and the geometrical clarity of James Silk Buckingham's (1786–1855) diagrammatic model city, Victoria. All were ingredients of Howard's 'unique combination of proposals', eventually published as *Tomorrow: A Peaceful Path to Real Reform* in 1898. It was a decade since *Looking Backward* – a progressive Utopian novel by Edward Bellamy (1850–98), visualising Boston in 2000, transformed by technology and cooperation – had alerted Howard to the 'splendid possibilities of a new civilisation based upon service to the community, and not on self-interest … I determined to take such part as I could, however small it might be, in helping to bring a new civilisation into being.'[3]

Howard assembled these disparate influences into a concept which was, at the same time, disarmingly simple but worryingly complex, idealistic yet pragmatic, grounded in business sense and promising a sustainable solution to contemporary problems. The solution was the garden city, which Howard believed would ensure a better environment for living in a rationally planned network of settlements. Any Utopianism was, however, underpinned by a corporate structure that would not only develop the community but also provide investment for the future benefit of its citizens.

How would garden cities be planned, built and maintained? Howard proposed that a private company, its constitution limiting annual dividends to 5 per cent, would raise capital to purchase a 6000-acre (2,428.1ha) estate of undeveloped agricultural land, to be held in trust for the residents of the future garden city. Development for homes and industry in enlightened physical form would increase the capital value of the enterprise, enhancing the ability to raise finance for phased progress towards completion. Trading surpluses, after payment of dividends, would be ploughed back for community benefit. Telling diagrams encapsulated his 'object lesson'. *The Three Magnets* (Fig 1) skilfully summarised urban and rural problems: in the town, opportunity, leisure, employment and relatively high wages were counterbalanced by environmental and moral problems, while in the country the benefits of fresh air and rural amenity were offset by social control and low wages. The solution lay in the irresistible attraction to the 'town-country' magnet, the garden city, vehicle of social reform, which offered the prospect of a fulfilling life in healthy surroundings and free from exploitation.

In considering the layout and architectural style of garden city settlements, Howard found little inspiration in the larger 19th-century new towns such as Barrow-in-Furness or Middlesborough. Although planned more or less from nothing, they were not an inspiring model for urban living, characterised as they were by monotonous grids of speculatively built terraced housing. The circular geometry of Howard's design model transposed the regulated squares of Buckingham's Victoria, although he pragmatically indicated that the final layout depended on the site selected. The urban centre would be limited to one-sixth of the land, with the remainder providing agricultural, institutional or recreational services for the community. Each garden city would contain six wards (Fig 2), forerunners of the neighbourhood unit. A central park with

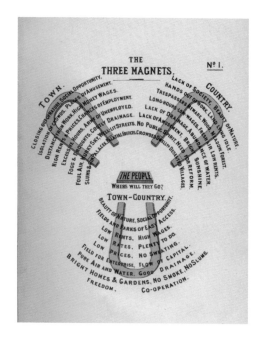

Figure 1
The Three Magnets, *in which Ebenezer Howard brilliantly summarised his concept of a 'joyous union' of town and country.*
[Hertfordshire Archives and Local Studies]

public buildings was bordered by a circular 'crystal palace' for shopping and commerce. Reminiscent of the Great Exhibition building of 1851 (Howard lived near its reincarnation at Sydenham), it also looked forward to 20th-century shopping malls. Howard drew upon earlier 19th-century developments such as Regent's Park or Bath, envisaging crescents and terraces strung along his broad circular 'Grand Avenue' with housing quadrangles elsewhere. The avenue's central greensward contained schools and churches. Around the perimeter of his garden city, an industrial estate benefited from technological advances, particularly electricity.

Each garden city would be limited to 32,000 residents and as near as possible self-sufficient. Ultimately six might form a regional 'social city' cluster round a larger central city, population 58,000, giving a total of 250,000, linked by radial roads and railways, but prevented from coalescence by agricultural belts (Fig 3). Howard's scheme, with its rational plan-based integration of all aspects of modern urban life and its marriage of town and country – together leading to his promised 'new civilisation' – presented a revolutionary contrast to Britain's crowded conurbations, developed piecemeal over centuries and seemingly unable to meet the challenge of contemporary problems.

Industrial villages

Howard's visionary ideas were drawn in part from earlier attempts to improve housing conditions in Britain's towns. Industrialists quickly learned the economic, social and advertising value of model housing. The Utopian, dour rectitude of Robert Owen's (1771–1858) New Lanark (begun 1798) had few literal successors, but by the 1860s housebuilding by employers had become widespread, especially in new railway towns such as Swindon, Crewe or Wolverton. West Yorkshire is notable for innovative settlements, including Saltaire (1853–63) and Akroydon (1861–73). At the former, Sir Titus Salt (1803–76) promoted rational integration of grid-layout terraces, differentiated to reflect the status of overseers and 'hands', with a mill the scale of a Renaissance palace, an evangelical church and a 'Sunday Best' park, all designed by the local architects Henry Francis Lockwood (1811–78) and William Mawson (1828–89), and all geared to maximising productivity.

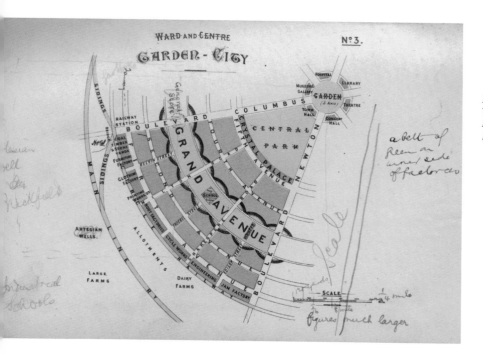

Figure 2
Ward and Centre, *1898. Proof copy with Ebenezer Howard's written amendments.*
[Hertfordshire Archives and Local Studies]

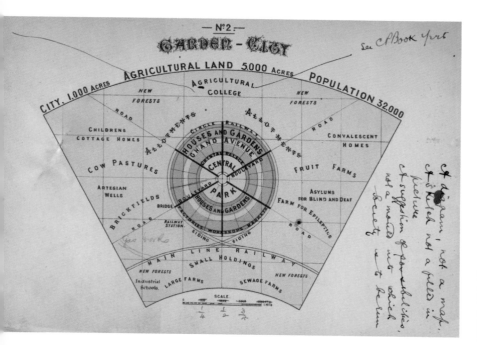

Figure 3
A proof copy of Garden City and Rural Belt, *1898. Ebenezer Howard's comments, bottom right, led to 'plan cannot be drawn until site selected', being added to the published version.*
[Hertfordshire Archives and Local Studies]

At the latter, Colonel Edward Akroyd (1810–87) retained Sir George Gilbert Scott (1811–78), most eminent of mid-Victorian Gothic Revivalist architects, indicative of the rising significance of aesthetics, although residents were unimpressed by his designs, which they claimed resembled almshouses. Throughout the late 19th century, company housing proliferated, ranging from a few dwellings to comprehensively planned communities, including shops, schools, institutes and churches – urban counterparts of estate villages built by wealthy landowners.

Arts and Crafts values

Advances in housing and civic design were influenced by a broader awareness of their social and economic context. Augustus Welby Northmore Pugin (1812–52), best remembered for clothing Sir Charles Barry's (1795–1860) Palace of Westminster in Gothic detail, held fanatical devotion to the Gothic Revival as his spiritual and moral compass, as reflected by his illustration in *Contrasts*, comparing an historic town of 1440 with its decayed and vandalised 1840 counterpart, where factory chimneys ousted broken spires – 'Coketown' manifest. Ruskin and Morris related aesthetic critique to socialist theory, prescribing universal dignity of labour, improved design and 'decency of surroundings'. Ruskin's call for houses 'in groups of limited extent … walled around … clean and busy streets within and open country without'[4] was taken up by architects of the Arts and Crafts Movement, in the corporate communities of Port Sunlight and Bournville, and subsequently the garden city.

Arts and Crafts architecture, defined through the work of Philip Webb (1831–60) and Richard Norman Shaw (1831–1912), was initially richly eclectic Old English revival or country Queen Anne. The latter style, with red brick walling and lively roof lines, blossomed at Bedford Park, a middle-class suburb developed in west London from 1875 onwards, where the layout preserved mature trees, providing an informal setting for houses designed by Shaw and his contemporaries. This harmony was disrupted in the 1890s by a revolutionary tall white roughcast house with stone mullioned windows, impudently commanding views across the village green: it was designed by C F A Voysey (1857–1941), whose architecture inspired much suburban and garden city housing.

Figure 4
*Port Sunlight, begun 1888. This aerial view highlights
the contrast between the cottage groups and the later
superimposed beaux-arts axial planning.*
[NMR/20746/021]

Two model villages also profoundly influenced 20th-century housing development: Port Sunlight,[5] on the Wirral west bank of the River Mersey (1888), and Bournville,[6] 8 km south-west of central Birmingham (1895). Their creators, William Hesketh Lever (1851–1925) and George Cadbury (1839–1922), both assisted the garden city to emerge from its theoretical chrysalis.

At Port Sunlight (Fig 4) Lever expanded his family grocery business into an industrial empire based upon Sunlight soap, brand leader by 1887. The following year he purchased a site north of his new Merseyside factory and

Figure 5 (above)
Corniche Road, Port Sunlight. The cottages in the middle distance were designed by Edwin Lutyens in 1897.
[Mervyn Miller]

Figure 6 (above, right)
The beaux-arts classicism of the Lady Leverhulme Art Gallery, Port Sunlight, 1910–22, by Segar Owen, with the base of the Leverhulme Memorial, 1930, by J Lomax Simpson.
[Mervyn Miller]

commenced building a village named to honour his most profitable product. Lever oversaw development with paternal pride, to realise 'a conveniently planned and healthy settlement laid out with all possible artistic thought on sound business lines'. He later built model housing at Thornton Hough, in the Wirral, near his country house. Lever's architects William Owen (1846–1910) and his son Segar Owen (b 1874) revived the black-and-white Cheshire vernacular architecture, a northern dimension of the Arts and Crafts Movement, which used beautifully crafted timber studwork above a stone base; a middle-class idealisation of working-class housing. Their contemporaries George Enoch Grayson (1833–1912) and Edward Augustus Lyle Ould (1852–1909) also designed prolifically. At Lever's bidding Flemish and other European styles were introduced. Further consultants were employed, including London-based architects such as Ernest Newton (1856–1922) and Edwin Lutyens (1869–1944). Open frontages ensured that individual shortcomings would not spoil the corporate image of the housing (Fig 5). Outbuildings and allotments were provided in the inner quadrangles away from public view. Port Sunlight seemed to be on parade. Lever realised the publicity value of his village, which was visited by politicians as well as English and European royalty. He became a benefactor of town planning in 1909, endowing Liverpool University's Chair in Civic Design. The following year a revised plan transformed Port Sunlight with beaux-arts formality. The creeks which had distorted the original layout were infilled, creating vistas for formal set pieces such as the Lady Leverhulme Art Gallery (Fig 6), the remarkable war memorial and the Congregational church.

Bournville reflected Cadbury's undemonstrative Quaker beliefs. In 1879, his chocolate factory was moved from the centre of Birmingham to Bournbrook, near Selly Oak. It was not until 1895 that Cadbury's architect William Alexander Harvey (1874–1951) planned the village, his designs influenced by Arts and Crafts architects, particularly Voysey and M H Baillie Scott (1865–1945). His informal terraced and semi-detached houses and cottages (Fig 7) rejected the self-conscious artiness of Port Sunlight, with designs which influenced New Earswick, Letchworth and the early London County Council cottage estates. The layout resembled a low-density suburb, with a central village green (Fig 8), shopping parade and nearby community buildings, such as the infant (Fig 9) and junior schools, the latter featuring a carillon, more integrated than Lever's set pieces. Cadbury encouraged families to grow their own fruit and vegetables. Up to half of the housing was available to non-Cadbury employees, which muted company paternalism and promoted social integration.

Figure 7 (below, left)
Semi-detached houses and cottages, Maryvale Road, Bournville, c 1900. The designs by William Alexander Harvey were strongly influenced by the Voysey idiom.
[Mervyn Miller]

Figure 8 (right)
Village Green, Bournville: The Rest House, 1914, by William Alexander Harvey and Herbert Graham Wicks commemorated the Silver Wedding of George and Elizabeth Cadbury. In the background is the shopping parade, 1908, by Henry Bedford Tylor.
[Mervyn Miller]

Figure 9 (below)
Infant school, Linden Road, Bournville, 1910, by William Alexander Harvey. Its benefactors were George and Elizabeth Cadbury.
[Mervyn Miller]

The co-partnership model

The co-partnership movement, founded in 1888, advocated an alternative to housing built by enlightened employers. It blended the 'five per cent philanthropy' of established agencies such as the Peabody Trust with a new idea – tenant participation. Tenants would purchase shares in a company formed to develop houses, which would be owned by the company or its corporate association, rather than by individuals. Dividends would be paid, and this gave tenants a stake in the success of the venture. By 1897 the movement had 17 offshoots. In 1900 Henry Vivian (1863–1930), carpenter and trade unionist, later Liberal MP, joined Ealing Tenants Ltd which operated in the western London suburbs. By September 1901, with £10,000 subscribed, its first nine houses, typical 'by-law' terraced types, were nearing completion in Brentham.[7] In January 1905 Vivian met Raymond Unwin (1863–1940), and all subsequent houses followed garden city standards, designed by Frederic Cavendish Pearson (1882–1963) (Fig 10) or George Lister Sutcliffe (1865–1915), the co-partners' architect. Co-partnership communities spread widely, with offshoots in Letchworth Garden City and Hampstead Garden Suburb.

Figure 10
Brunner Road, Brentham, c *1910, is typical of the inventive street pictures designed by Frederic Cavendish Pearson.*
[Brentham Society Archives]

Gathering momentum

Howard's 1898 book contributed to the debate about provision of innovative housing, attracting attention and scepticism in equal measure. The Garden City Movement needed the means to translate words into action. The Garden City Association was formed in June 1899, aspiring to build a demonstration of Howard's 'object lesson'.[8] In 1901, the association's credibility was enhanced by recruitment of Ralph Neville (1865–1930), an eminent barrister who soon became chairman, and Thomas Adams (1870–1940), a Scots surveyor interested in rural regeneration, as secretary. Cadbury hosted the association's conference at Bournville in September 1901, a landmark both for the movement and the emergence of town planning. Not to be upstaged, Lever followed suit at Port Sunlight in July 1902. By then the Garden City Pioneer Company was registered with £20,000 capital, to identify and purchase a suitable site. Howard's book was revised and reprinted as *Garden Cities of Tomorrow*, by which title it became universally known.

Translating vision into reality: Parker and Unwin

The layout and housing design of the early garden city settlements are most closely associated with Barry Parker (1867–1947) and Unwin. Parker was articled to G Faulkner Armitage (1849–1937), a northern Arts and Crafts architect with a studio at Altrincham, Cheshire. Unwin, born in Yorkshire, grew up in Oxford (where he heard lectures by Ruskin and Morris) and then returned northwards, trained as a mining engineer and developed political skills as Manchester Branch Secretary of Morris's Socialist League. Both were enthusiastic devotees of the Arts and Crafts Movement, and in 1896 they came together to form a partnership in Buxton, Derbyshire. They collaborated in writing *The Art of Building a Home* (1901), which extended the domestic realm into co-operative housing, setting out themes reflected in their garden city community designs, with which Unwin, especially, was involved.

In September 1901 Unwin's briefing paper for garden city housing, delivered at the Bournville conference, led in 1902 to a commission for

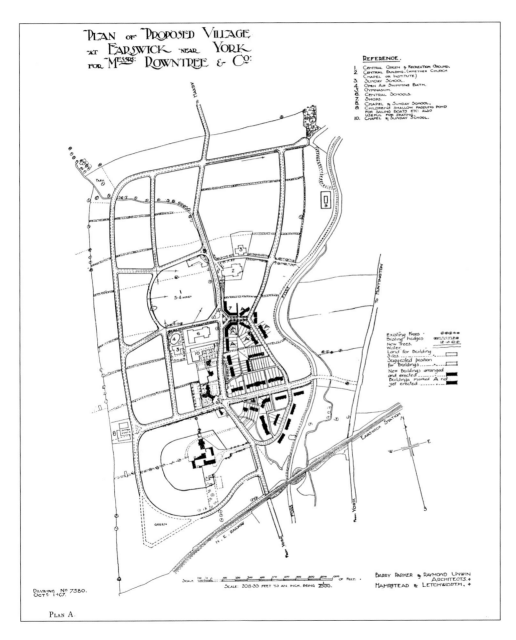

Figure 11
New Earswick, York, promoted by the Joseph Rowntree Village Trust. The layout and design, from 1902, gave Barry Parker and Raymond Unwin valuable experience of housing layout. [Nettlefold 1908, Fold Plan A]

a plan for New Earswick (Fig 11), near York,[9] where Joseph Rowntree (1836–1925), the Quaker chocolate manufacturer, was emulating Cadbury's model community on the outskirts of the city. This became a testing ground for garden city design standards: Unwin's plan for the first phase of development (1902–6) included housing of gabled paired and grouped cottages in a simplified Voysey style (Fig 12). Although only 26 cottages had been completed by December 1904, their designs enabled 'variations on a theme' to be utilised at Letchworth. Likewise, the Folk Hall closely resembled the Mrs Howard Memorial Hall at Letchworth. Later, in 1919, Parker was appointed for the inter-war development at New Earswick, and his rationalised cottages and closes paralleled his local authority work and planning for Wythenshawe.

Figure 12
Western Terrace, New Earswick, 1902–3: group cottage prototypes for Letchworth.
[© First Garden City Heritage Museum]

2

Masterplanning the garden city communities

Three places – Letchworth and Welwyn Garden Cities and Hampstead Garden Suburb – represent the most comprehensive realisation of Ebenezer Howard's ideas. All resulted from the idealism of committed visionary individuals – Howard himself at Letchworth and Welwyn and Henrietta Barnett at Hampstead – who skilfully recruited like-minded yet influential and pragmatic colleagues able to carry the schemes towards implementation. In each case the development vehicle was a privately funded limited liability company, albeit with a voluntary dividend restriction, following the 'five per cent philanthropy' model. Each was begun when possession of land freehold carried the unfettered right to develop, with minimum regulation from local authorities. Letchworth Garden City and Hampstead Garden Suburb provided such potent demonstrations of the benefits of enlightened development that they influenced the adoption of their standards and principles through statutory town planning, which emerged in 1909 to be administered, initially on an optional basis, by local authorities representing the corporate expression of public interest.

Howard's formal circular layout may have suggested a radial centrepiece at Letchworth, to which Raymond Unwin added informal perimeter 'villages' on the scale of New Earswick. If the informal Arts and Crafts architecture of Letchworth belied the formal framework around the centre, the systematic grouping of houses and the spatial design around road junctions at Hampstead Garden Suburb produced a more integrated townscape. Unwin's initial layout had been self-consciously informal (based upon his misreading of Camillo Sitte's manual on urban design), but was tightened into a geometric layout for the artisans' housing, while the loose-knit village-style centre was superseded by the civic grandeur of Edwin Lutyens' (1869–1944) central squares. The more consistent acceptance of Queen Anne and neo-Georgian architectural models provided the basis for Welwyn Garden City, arguably the most sophisticated of the three seminal plans. Louis de Soissons (1890–1962) balanced the formalism of the town centre with the sweeping Parkway axis (one of the finest 20th-century townscapes) and intimate, informal housing areas. During the first two decades of the 20th century physical planning of new communities emerged, via the Garden City Movement, as one of the key British contributions to the international development of urban planning. An important component of this was the 1919 Housing Act, much stronger than

The sinews of the Parker and Unwin layout for Letchworth, the first garden city, stand out on this aerial photograph from 2009. [NMR/26529/029]

17

its 1909 predecessor. Under it, local authorities themselves became statutory developers of the municipalised garden city, through provision of central Government subsidised working-class housing, designed along garden city lines. This occurred just as development of Howard's second garden city at Welwyn began. One of the most comprehensive expositions of the municipal garden suburb is at Wythenshawe, Greater Manchester.

Letchworth: the first garden city

The Garden City Pioneer Company examined several sites. It had virtually settled on Chartley Castle, near Stafford, when in April 1903 the Letchworth Hall estate, near Hitchin, Hertfordshire, became available (Fig 13). It amounted to only 1,014 acres (410.3ha), but nearby land was acquired to give a total of 3,818 acres (1,545ha). First Garden City Ltd was registered in September 1903 and the following month, in a marquee south of Baldock Road, with pouring rain lashing the canvas, Earl Grey declared the estate open: appropriately the location is now named Muddy Lane. A limited competition for the layout plan brought entries from William Richard Lethaby (1857–1931) and Halsey Ricardo (1854–1928); Geoffry Lucas (1872–1947) and Sidney Cranfield (1870–1961); and Barry Parker and Raymond Unwin, who submitted the winning plan, endorsed by the company in February 1904. Parker and Unwin were retained by First Garden City Ltd and their influence was pervasive both in implementing the plan and in detailed design (Fig 14).

The garden city estate was bisected by the Hitchin to Cambridge branch of the Great Northern Railway (now the East Coast Main Line), crossed by the Hitchin to Baldock Road to the south, and the Norton to Wilbury Road to the north. The master plan, published in April 1904, initially suggests paperwork geometry with major and minor axes. Resemblance between Unwin's town centre and the Exchange area on Sir Christopher Wren's plan for rebuilding the City of London after the Great Fire of 1666 notwithstanding, the layout was carefully related to topography. The factory estate sited itself either side of the railway in the north-east of the site. The station was in the town centre, above the Pix valley, along which Norton Way, the principal new north–south road, ran beside meadows, which became Howard Park. The town centre site, west of Norton Way South, was an open, level plateau, with a line through a distant, angled copse south-west to Hitchin Road, which fixed the line of Broadway. From the centre (now Broadway Gardens) a web of roads radiated outwards. Housing areas were informally treated: those east of Norton Way South,

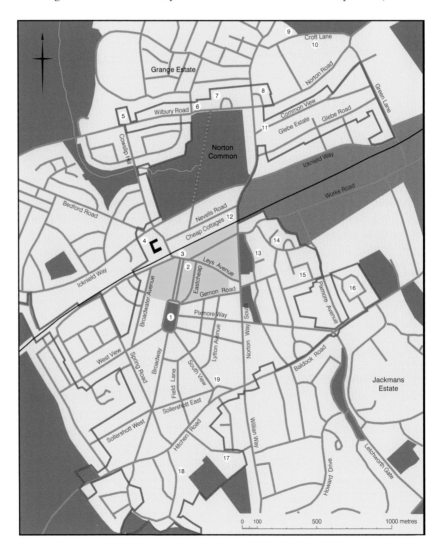

Figure 13
Map of Letchworth: the first garden city.

Key

1. Broadway Gardens
2. Old Estate Office
3. Station
4. Spirella
5. Stanley Parker House
6. 158 Wilbury Road
7. Westholm
8. Eastholm
9. The White Cottage
10. Three Gables
11. St George's Church
12. The Settlement
13. Rushby Mead
14. Birds Hill
15. Pixmore Estate
16. Jackman's Place
17. The Cloisters
18. Dean Row
19. Howgills

Conservation Area
Railways
Town Centre
Industrial and Business

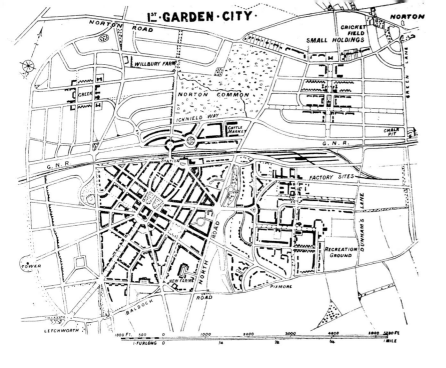

Figure 14
The Parker and Unwin layout for Letchworth, first
published in spring 1904.
[Purdom 1913, 42]

convenient for the industrial area, were developed with working-class housing,
while close to Broadway were lower-density zones of larger individual houses.

In 1904, Unwin drafted the company's Building Regulations, a pioneer of
its kind, including aesthetic and technical matters. 'Simple and straightforward
building' with 'the use of good and harmonious materials' was commended;
'useless ornamentation' was discouraged.[10] Pebbledashed or painted roughcast
brickwork walls and tiled roofs became almost standard, particularly for
grouped housing, and slate was embargoed. Unwin considered that the local
yellow-grey Arlesey bricks looked poor: however, red brick was approved and
used on larger houses and public buildings. As an exemplar, the Parker and
Unwin office on Norton Way South, 1907 (Fig 15), took the form of a thatched
vernacular hall house in which the 'solar', Parker's private office, had a 'squint'
window through which he kept a watchful eye over the drawing office.

Circumstances compromised the idealistic vision for the garden city
as a commercial venture. Thomas Adams, the estate manager, and his
successor, Walter Gaunt (1871–1951), prioritised the attraction of industry.
Demonstration of Howard's 'object lesson' required financial returns in
addition to social and environmental benefits. At times opportunism appeared
uppermost: an early instance, the 1905 Cheap Cottages Exhibition – a
worthy idea designed to demonstrate how poorer families could be housed

Figure 15
The romantic idealism manifested in the Parker and
Unwin office, 296 Norton Way South, 1907. It was opened
as the First Garden City [Heritage] Museum in 1973.
[Mervyn Miller]

at reasonable cost – lacked visual coordination. Consequently, Letchworth attained an unenvisaged diversity, with speculative builders' designs alongside work by eminent architects.

The incremental building of the town centre fell short of the 'master plan' aspiration. Commercial development proceeded along Leys Avenue and Station Road, and the construction of Eastcheap, one of the major shopping streets, was delayed for several years. On the south side of Leys Avenue the 1907–8 shopping parades by Robert Bennett (1878–1956) and Wilson Bidwell (1877–1944) were mixed Queen Anne style, with Arts and Crafts touches: their early 1920s Midland Bank – turning the corner from Leys Avenue to Station Road – the adjoining parades and the entrances to 'The Arcade' were more classically inclined.

Public buildings were formal, carried out in dark red brick, early Georgian style. The Estate Office, Broadway, 1912–13 (Fig 16); Museum, Broadway Gardens, 1914; and rebuilt Free Church, Norton Way South, 1923 – the last with a green Westmoreland slate roof – reflected the influence

Figure 16
First Garden City Ltd, Estate Office, Broadway, Letchworth, 1912–13, by Parker and Unwin. A Lutyens-influenced prototype for later civic buildings.
[DP088199]

of Lutyens' centrepiece at Hampstead Garden Suburb. While Town Square was laid out, it was destined never to receive the central civic and religious buildings, modelled 'on the works of Wren and other masters', shown in a 1912 perspective sketch (Fig 17). Lombardy Poplars were planted to define the buildings' outline; these were eventually felled during remodelling of the square as Broadway Gardens in 2003, Letchworth's centenary year. Only the west side of the square, with the former Grammar School (Parker, 1931), had a sense of visual cohesion. Bennett and Bidwell designed the Queen Anne-style former council offices, built in 1935 on the north side of the square.

Tree-planting and landscaping were essential elements of the garden city image. Only one tree was felled in laying out the plan. Norton Common was incorporated without development. The trees and greenswards of the residential roads unified variable building standards. Hedges, trees, shrubs and verges gave the whole town a park-like appearance befitting the term 'garden city' (Fig 18). Outside the defined town area (and within until the land was required for development) the original farms were leased out, with the objective of providing food for the community. The reservation of an agricultural belt, often considered to anticipate the 1950s green belts, was a voluntary undertaking by First Garden City Ltd.

Can Letchworth's many achievements be heralded as a successful demonstration of the garden city ideal? Town and country integrated in Howard's 'joyous union'; pioneer functional land-use zoning to define residential, industrial and amenity areas; a maximum of 12 houses to the acre; clear definition of building standards; tree-lined roads and generous open spaces – all were tangible benefits. Grouping houses into identifiable community units evolved through Eastholm, Westholm, Birds Hill, Pixmore, the Glebe Estate and Rushby Mead. Theory and plan were in accord, but implementation posed problems, as for subsequent new towns. Under-capitalisation made for slow progress, and, as we have seen, commercial development disappointed original expectations. Perhaps the biggest discrepancy between plan and execution was the failure to build an identifiable civic core befitting the status of the first garden city. Some disruption may have resulted from Unwin's departure in 1906 to plan Hampstead Garden Suburb, although the joint consultancy lasted until 1914. Parker continued alone until 1943, four years before his death.

Figure 17
Town Square, now Broadway Gardens, Letchworth. A 1912 aspirational perspective of Raymond Unwin's concept, modelled 'on the works of Wren and other masters'.
[Mervyn Miller]

Figure 18
Aerial view of Letchworth Garden City in 2009, looking north along the Broadway axis: the low density housing south of Sollershott West, Broadway, and in The Glade has attained an Arcadian setting.
[NMR/26530/009]

The suburb salubrious: Hampstead Garden Suburb

As the 19th century turned into the 20th, London rapidly sprawled outwards, through the development and extension of the suburban and underground railways. Suburban living and central London employment became a possibility for many, and districts such as Tottenham, Willesden and Acton grew swiftly, laid out with 'by-law' terraces. Electric traction made deep underground lines practicable. In 1902, parliamentary sanction was granted for building the Charing Cross, Euston and Hampstead railway (now part of the Northern Line) running beneath Hampstead village to Golders Green, with a proposed (but never completed) station at Wyldes, off North End Road. This area, north of Hampstead Heath, was largely farmland, and the rural Golders Green crossroads on the Finchley Road was now ripe for development. In 1907 David Lloyd George (1863–1945), President of the Board of Trade, opened Golders Green Station (Fig 19).

Henrietta Barnett was an important 19th-century reformer (Fig 20).[11] Although from a wealthy family, she became an assistant to and was profoundly influenced by Octavia Hill, pioneer of social work and leader of London common land preservation. Henrietta married Samuel Augustus Barnett (1844–1913), a long-serving vicar of Whitechapel, who opened the first university settlement house at Toynbee Hall in 1884. The Whitechapel slums were among the most densely populated East End districts. The Barnetts laboured to bring spiritual, moral and social enlightenment to the poor of the parish. They had a weekend retreat on the northern fringe of Hampstead Heath, renamed St Jude's Cottage, after Samuel's Whitechapel church. They became acutely concerned about the impact of the new tube line. Combining altruism with self-interest, Mrs Barnett began campaigning to preserve an extension to Hampstead Heath below St Jude's Cottage.

The 323-acre (130.7ha) Wyldes Farm had been owned by Eton College since 1531: its timber-framed farmhouse survived from the 17th century. Seeking an option to purchase, Mrs Barnett approached the college bursar to be told that she was 'only a woman', advising her to enhance her credibility by recruiting men of standing and influence. She formed her 'syndicate of eight': two earls, two lawyers, two free churchmen, a bishop, and a woman (herself). Thus the Hampstead Heath Protection Committee was formed, later the nucleus of the Hampstead Garden Suburb Trust. Influenced by publicity about the First Garden City Estate at Letchworth, Mrs Barnett added 'a garden suburb for all classes' to her campaign, with the Heath Extension as an internal green reservation. She began fundraising and commissioned Unwin to prepare a preliminary plan (although it appeared under the practice name of Parker and Unwin). In the 1880s he had consulted Samuel Barnett about studying for Holy Orders, but instead had pursued his reforming zeal through the Garden City Movement.

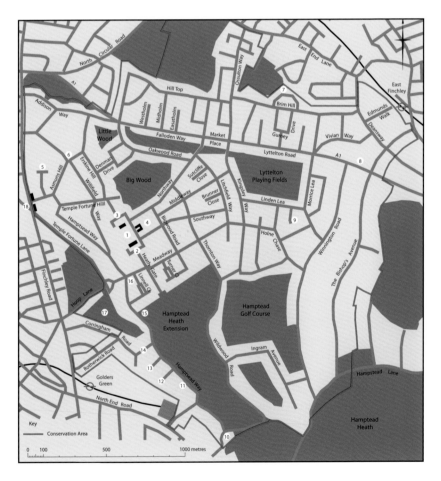

Figure 19
Map of Hampstead Garden Suburb.

Key

1. Central Square
2. St Jude's Church
3. the Free Church
4. Henrietta Barnett School (formerly the Institute)
5. Asmuns Place
6. site of the Club House
7. Howard Walk
8. Belvedere Court
9. Lytton Close
10. Wyldes
11. Heathcroft
12. Reynolds Close
13. Heath Close and Waterlow Court
14. Corringham Road squares
15. the Great Wall
16. Baillie Scott Corner
17. Golders Green Crematorium
18. Temple Fortune gateway

Figure 20
Henrietta Barnett, founder of Hampstead Garden Suburb, photographed in her 30s. Her many achievements were recognised by the award of DBE in 1924.
[London Metropolitan Archives]

Wyldes Farm was conveyed to the Hampstead Garden Suburb Trust on 1 May 1907. The next day Mrs Barnett dug the turf for the foundations of the first cottages, to be built on Hampstead Way, proclaiming regally that the lands of Henry VIII had been conveyed to '… Henrietta Octavia, a woman and not a queen, but for many years a 'general servant' in Whitechapel – buying them with the money of democracy for the homes of democracy'.[12]

Unwin's preliminary plan (Fig 21), signed with Mrs Barnett's enthusiastic comments, included neighbourhoods with housing of differing size and status to fulfil her objective of accommodating all classes assigned to discrete areas – 'a place for everyone' with 'everyone in their place'. The western boundary of the suburb ran along Finchley Road and Temple Fortune Lane, crossing Hoop Lane, then along Wild Hatch, behind North End Road to Wyldes farmhouse and returned north, east of the proposed Heath Extension, across a plateau, which would eventually be graced with the central squares. The 'Artisans' Quarter' on the north-west of the site, behind Finchley Road, was Unwin's masterpiece of housing layout and design, respecting old field boundaries, preserving virtually every tree, and some hedgerows (Fig 22). Private legislation – the Hampstead Garden Suburb Act, 1906 – enabled the suburb

Figure 22
Hampstead Garden Suburb from the Heath Extension by Annie Walker. *This classic view culminates in the crowning glory of Lutyens' buildings in the central squares.*
[Annie Walker, Mervyn Miller and BJP Photographic]

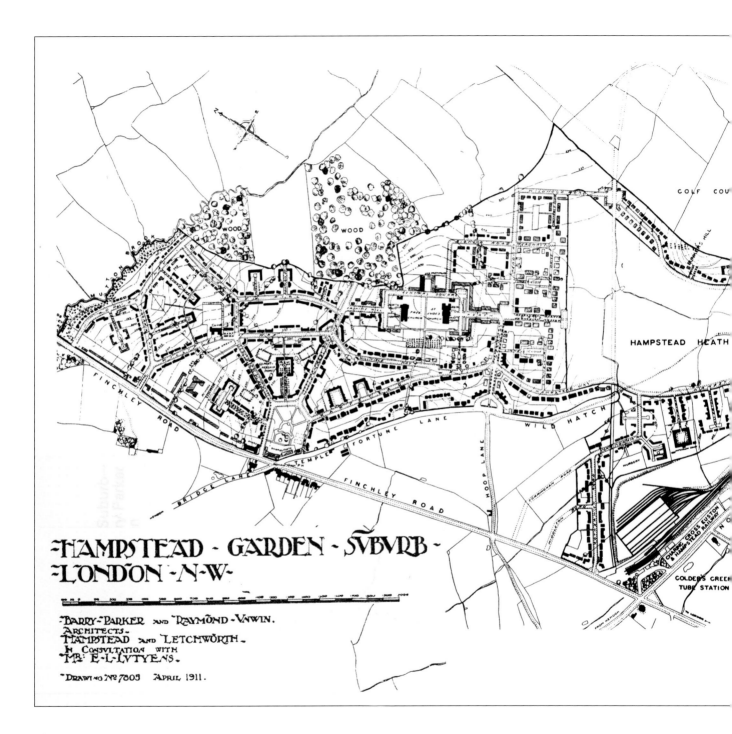

HAMPSTEAD · GARDEN · SVBVRB ·
LONDON · N·W·

BARRY · PARKER AND RAYMOND · VNWIN.
ARCHITECTS ·
HAMPSTEAD AND LETCHWORTH ·
IN CONSVLTATION WITH
MR · E·L·LVTYENS.

DRAWING Nº 7805 APRIL 1911.

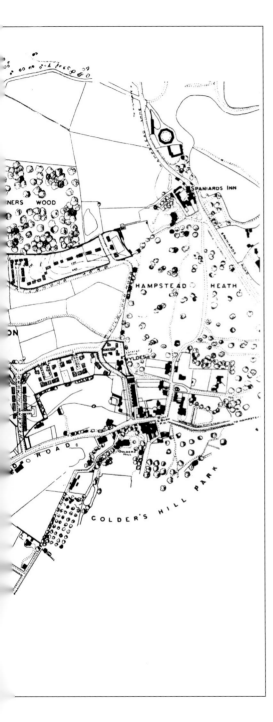

Figure 21
The 'definitive' Parker and Unwin drawing of
the layout for Hampstead Garden Suburb, 1911,
incorporates Lutyens' layout for the central
squares.
[Unwin 1911, Fold Map VI]

to benefit from lightly paved roads, cul-de-sacs and preservation of natural features.

Unwin admired the historic walled hill towns of southern Germany. To define the northern boundary of the Heath Extension, he proposed a wall, studded with pavilions and gazebos, which was detailed by his assistant Charles Paget Wade (1882–1956). The 'Great Wall' leads to a piazza, Sunshine Corner, linking the Heath Extension with the central square by an axial vista. In 1906 Lutyens, then a rising star renowned for his country houses, was appointed joint consultant with Unwin. His developing taste for the Grand Manner (which would culminate in Imperial New Delhi) was applied to the central squares (Fig 23) and their approaches. Between 1907 and 1910 Lutyens cast aside Unwin's 'village' groupings and a central Trinity emerged:

Figure 23
The central squares, Hampstead Garden Suburb, 2009. Aerial view with the Free Church, the former Institute and St Jude's, looking towards the 'New Suburb', planned by Raymond Unwin in 1911.
[NMR/26445/040]

two churches – St Jude's and the Free Church – framing the Institute (now the Henrietta Barnett School). Although the churches are related in design, they differ in their skylines. St Jude's, with its spire, followed the outline of a traditional Gothic church, but its eclectic interior ranged from Arts and Crafts to Classicism. The Free Church, funded by the Baptists, has a low, rather Byzantine, dome. It has a more consistently Classical interior, using Lutyens's favourite Tuscan Doric columns. Framed between the churches, the Institute evolved over many years, and Lutyens changed its design more than once. With its cupola, and crisply detailed grey brickwork, with red dressings, it has a rather Colonial Williamsburg character.

The open westward view towards Harrow church from Central Square was a favourite of Mrs Barnett. After her death in 1936 the ingenious arched memorial to her, designed by Lutyens, was sited to command that view. North and South Squares and their approaches contain houses of Lutyens' style, but not always designed by him. Heathgate and South Square are largely by John Carrick Stuart Soutar (1881–1951) and Arthur Stanley George Butler (1888–1955). However, Nos 1–8 North Square and Nos 1–7 (odd) Erskine Hill are original Lutyens designs, but the remainder of North Square and the even numbers on Erskine Hill were by George Lister Sutcliffe, the co-partners' architect.

Around the perimeter boundary there were several architectural 'gateways'. The most imposing is at Temple Fortune (Fig 24), where Hampstead Way emerges on to Finchley Road. This is emphasised by two tall dark-brown brick buildings, containing shops with flats above. Arcade House and Temple Fortune House were designed in Unwin's office in 1909–11 by Arthur Joseph Penty (1875–1937), a Guild Socialist, who exploited the picturesque character of the designs and incorporated one of Unwin's favourite Germanic towers as an eye-catcher on the Hampstead Way flank of Temple Fortune House.

Hampstead Garden Suburb was transformed in 1911–12 by the acquisition of a further 412 acres (166.7ha) to the east, which allowed a significant extension, known as the 'New Suburb'. Linking old and new, Little Wood and Big Wood were preserved in their natural state. Denman Drive, with excellent housing designed by Sutcliffe, was developed in 1912, but the major housebuilding occurred in the inter-war period. The main roads in the

Figure 24
The Hampstead Way gateway group at Temple Fortune, 1909–11, viewed from Finchley Road was designed by Arthur Joseph Penty in Raymond Unwin's office. [DP110937]

New Suburb – Northway, Middleway and Southway – were thrust eastwards from Central Square in Unwin's preliminary layout, which had been sketched on board a ship en route to a conference in the United States in May 1911. A major road across the north, Addison Way, was developed just before the First World War. During the 1920s the Ministry of Transport built new arterial roads in north-west London, including the Barnet bypass. Unfortunately, the eastern section of Addison Way was commandeered, renamed Lyttelton Road and Falloden Way, and channelled increasing volumes of traffic through the north of the 'New Suburb', increasing the isolation of the inter-war housing over towards East Finchley.

How did the Garden Suburb match up to Howard's vision? The hardline view was that it diluted the ideal with an easy option, reducing to the scale of a mere suburb what was envisaged as a self-contained alternative to the contemporary city. But Hampstead could equally well be regarded as a model for application of garden city principles to the expansion of existing towns to bring social and environmental gains. The formidable achievement of integrated high-quality architecture and Arcadian roads and open spaces brought Sir Nikolaus Pevsner's oft-quoted plaudit of the Suburb as 'the most nearly perfect example of the unique English invention and speciality – the Garden Suburb'.[13] As early as 1909, the year which saw the birth of statutory town planning in England, Unwin emphasised its aesthetic values in his seminal text *Town Planning in Practice*, and in 1912 defined the contrast with the harsh streetscapes of conventional London suburbs in *Nothing Gained by Overcrowding* – his case for lower-density development. Factors beyond Mrs Barnett's control made impracticable her objective of housing all social classes, which was engulfed by the rising tide of property prices and the dominance of owner occupation from the 1930s onwards. Residence is now effectively the preserve of the affluent. In summary, while Hampstead Garden Suburb represented the architectural ideals of the Garden City Movement to perfection, in planning terms it fell short of attaining Howard's comprehensive vision, being somewhat two-dimensional, restricted to institutional and residential elements, and lacking provision for local employment. Its size – much smaller than the garden cities – and its situation on the fringe of the capital, with easy access to employment in the city, were responsible for its physical form and social profile.

Welwyn Garden City

In 1919 Howard, nearing 70, and his younger supporters in the Garden Cities and Town Planning Association, Sir Frederic Osborn (1885–1978) and Charles Benjamin Purdom (1883–1965), were disappointed by the Government's neutral stance over garden cities compared to the generous grants and compulsion for local authority housing, albeit that development along garden city lines was required. Howard had told Osborn that he knew the ideal location for the second garden city – near Welwyn, an historic Hertfordshire town on the Great North Road, 32km north of central London – and during 1918 he took Osborn and Purdom to walk across the site. Most of the land belonged to Lord Desborough's Panshanger estate and was put up for auction in May 1919. The association initially balked at a second privately developed garden city – at Letchworth it would take many years to pay off the dividend arrears – but several of Howard's supporters rallied round with loans to meet a deposit of £3,000 (it actually required a further £250 from Norman Savill, Howard's agent at the auction). With 1,458 acres (590ha) in hand, an additional 230 acres (93ha) acquired by agreement, and 689 acres (278.8ha) shortly afterwards purchased from Lord Salisbury (1864–1958), planning went ahead (Fig 25).

The major part of the site was a plateau, divided by the Great Northern Railway, with branch lines westward to Dunstable and eastward to Hertford (both long-since closed). Osborn prepared a provisional layout (Fig 26), with the town centre to the west, south of the curving Dunstable line and major residential areas to the east. Hope of an integrated layout was dashed by the railway's requirement of a 650ft wayleave. A second sketch layout by Courtenay Melville Crickmer (1879–1971) ratified the location of industry on the east, but was abandoned in favour of a definitive master plan (Fig 27) by de Soissons. Of French Canadian background, trained at the Royal Academy in London and the École de Beaux Arts in Paris, he was appointed consultant architect to Welwyn Garden City Ltd in April 1920 and presented his plan in June. It featured formal planning on two axes – Parkway, parallel to the railway, and Howardsgate at right angles, leading to the station – and created sweeping lines, complemented by civilised and often inventive neo-Georgian buildings, many by de Soissons' practice. A semi-circular exedra, practically tucked

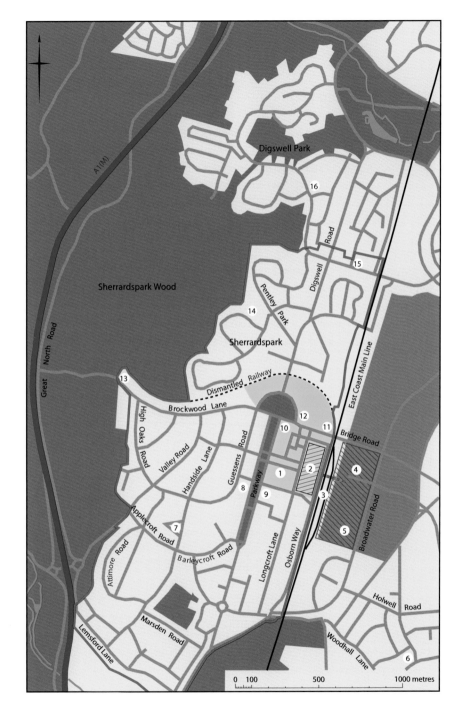

Figure 25
Map of Welwyn Garden City.

Key

1. Howardsgate
2. Howard Centre
3. Station
4. Shredded Wheat Factory
5. Roche Products
6. Woodhall Community Centre
7. Ideal Home Model Village
8. St Francis's Church
9. the Free Church
10. John Lewis
11. Waitrose (The Cherry Tree)
12. Council offices
13. Badgers End
14. Templewood School
15. Knightsfield Flats
16. Church of Holy Family

——— Conservation Area
▬▬▬ Motorways
——— Railways

Town Centre

Industrial and Business

Regeneration for mixed uses

Howard Centre

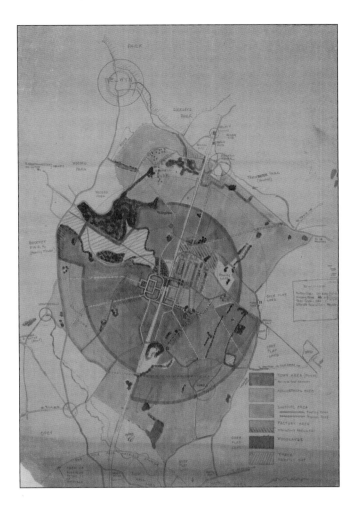

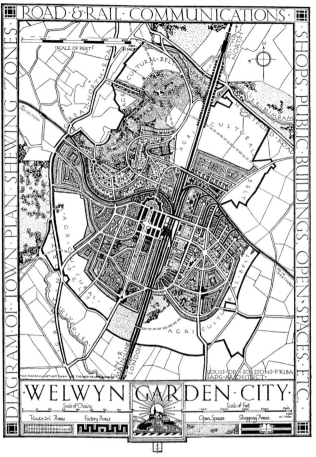

Figure 26
Sketch plan for Welwyn Garden City, 1919, by Sir Frederic Osborn: the first tentative attempt to plan Ebenezer Howard's second garden city.
[© Margaret Fenton/Town & Country Planning Association]

Figure 27
The 'definitive' plan, 1920, by Louis de Soissons established the framework for development with its axial centre and informal neighbourhoods.
[Purdom 1925, 205]

against the curve of the Dunstable branch line, created space for an incremental civic centre (now known as The Campus), while an informal approach was taken to the residential neighbourhoods westward. Industry bordered the east of the railway, initially with private sidings. Further east still were residential neighbourhoods, creating the impression of 'a wrong side of the tracks'.

Welwyn Garden City Ltd was floated in April 1920. Sir Theodore Chambers

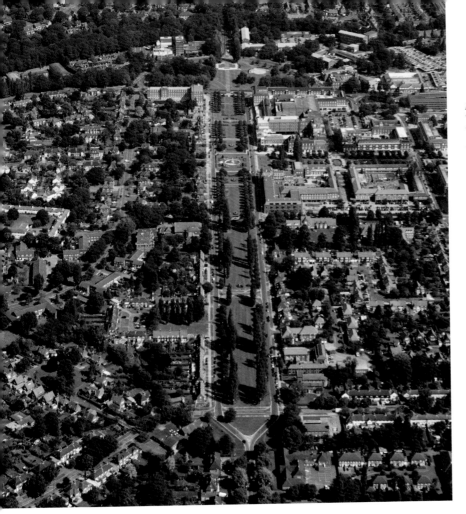

Figure 28
The Parkway axis, looking north to The Campus, 2009.
The town centre is to the right, in the middle distance.
[NMR/26434/010]

(1871–1957), Controller of War Savings, was appointed chairman and astutely piloted the project through difficult economic conditions. As at Letchworth, growth was initially slow, as Welwyn Garden City Ltd was under-subscribed, and the directors personally guaranteed the venture up to £95,000. The company ambitiously created subsidiaries dedicated to housing, building, electricity, horticulture, gravel and sand, brickmaking, transport, central stores and public houses. Howard's original concept provided for company development of shops, which had not been financially viable at Letchworth. At Welwyn, the company imposed a 10-year embargo on private shops and opened the Welwyn Stores in 1921. This postponed building of the shopping centre along Howardsgate until the late 1920s and consolidation along

Stonehills until after the Second World War. In contrast, housing development proceeded more rapidly, aided by the success in attracting new industry to the garden city. By 1926, 1,818 houses had been built, and the garden city had a population of 13,500 by 1938.

How does Welwyn rank in the hierarchy of garden cities? It was able to benefit from earlier experience at Letchworth and its site brought advantages of greater accessibility to and from London. Its plan and development perhaps most fully represented Howard's concept of functional zoning and the ideal of the city, which, while not self-sufficient, provided a full range of facilities in a rationally planned environment. Landscaping is a highlight: the broad expanse and sweeping vistas of Parkway (Fig 28) must have astonished contemporaries used to the cramped irregularities of English town centres, and the residential areas combine architectural finesse with a verdant setting. For many years the fleeting glance of the Shredded Wheat Factory afforded railway passengers a landmark of local identity. Development stuttered, and ideological and commercial issues, particularly shopping provision, caused friction. Nevertheless, Welwyn Garden City grew and prospered during the inter-war years. Whether its success was, and remains, due to its convenience for London commuters, is a moot point. Its achievement in building a genuinely new city was, however, of huge importance in influencing later experiments in town planning: it was the conduit through which Howard's garden city ideas flowed into the post-war era of reconstruction, of which Welwyn Garden City itself became a significant part.

Death of Howard

Despite his age, Howard (Fig 29) had enthusiastically observed the development of Welwyn Garden City. He lived with his second wife in a modest house in Guessens Road. In his spare time he continued to refine his 'phonoplayer', the shorthand typewriter which he was convinced would ultimately fund a third garden city. Knighted in 1927, he fell ill in spring 1928, died in May and was buried in Letchworth. His most appropriate memorial, apart from the two garden cities, rests in Howardsgate – a handsome bronze relief plaque by James Woodward (*see* Fig 104).

Figure 29
Newly knighted in 1927, Ebenezer Howard sits for a portrait bust by Ivy Young.
[Hertfordshire Archives and Local Studies]

3

Garden city homes

The garden city revolutionised housing standards: Sir Frederic Osborn emphasised its achievement of democratisation of design. The Arts and Crafts Movement had reformed the 'smaller middle-class' house during the 1890s, and this had been extended by the tied cottages of Port Sunlight, Bournville and New Earswick.

Cottages for artisans

Through development by the co-partnership tenants and other like providers, particularly the Howard Cottage Society at Letchworth, significant amounts of artisans' housing was built at Letchworth and Hampstead Garden Suburb. The delicate balancing act between cost and rent, however, placed such housing beyond the means of many labourers, particularly at the latter. At Welwyn Garden City, the situation was different. The 1919 Housing Act had placed a statutory duty on local authorities to provide working-class housing on garden city lines, assisted by generous Government subsidies. The Welwyn Rural District Council and its successor, Welwyn Garden City Urban District Council, participated in construction, and Second Garden City Ltd was also recognised as a public utility society for housebuilding. At Letchworth the Housing Act enabled the newly created Letchworth Urban District Council to build several fine 'cottage' estates in the early 1920s.

The private sector developed more incrementally, particularly at Letchworth, where contractors were small, and until the inter-war period proceeded plot by plot. Only in Hampstead Garden Suburb was municipal housing absent. It did, however, show significant achievement in coordinating design control for private sector construction. The Garden Suburb Development Company, founded in 1907 to build new houses and to promote design in the suburb, ran a programme of 120 houses in Willifield Way in 1908–9, carried out by a contractor from Loughborough, Leicestershire. The co-partners too organised their own contractors, who were fully occupied with the original Artisans' Quarter at the same period.

Innovation in housing design and construction was promoted through exhibitions in the early years of both garden cities, with mixed results but extensive publicity. Indeed, the on-site show house originated there. The

House on Dognell Green, Welwyn Garden City, shows the elegant simplicity of inter-war designs by Louis de Soissons.
[DP088351]

exhibitions featured innovatory design and building techniques, impelled by the search for economy in construction. At Letchworth the Cheap Cottage Exhibition of 1905 – whose objective was to demonstrate that sound housing could be provided for £150 per dwelling, net of land cost – was promoted by *The County Gentleman* and *Spectator periodicals*.[14] It was estimated that 60,000 visitors came, many via the special fare from King's Cross. The majority of the sites were in Exhibition (now Nevells) Road (Fig 30), The Quadrant, Cross Street and Icknield Way, with more isolated plots along Wilbury Road and a small estate on a green between Birds Hill and the railway.

In spite of doubts about building standards and experimental techniques, most exhibits survive today (Fig 31): No 217 Icknield Way, prizewinner in Class I, was designed by Percy Bond Houfton (d 1926), an architect friend of Raymond Unwin's from Derbyshire; No 221, the prizewinning wooden cottage, was by Robert Bennett and Wilson Bidwell, former assistants of Parker and Unwin, who had just formed their own practice (Bennett and Bidwell); No 245, a vernacular jettied-fronted cottage was by Oswald Partidge Milne (1881–1968), who had just left Edwin Lutyens' office. Other exhibits showed that use of innovative materials need not produce poor design. No 4 Cross Street, designed by Gilbert Wilson Fraser (1873–1954), judged best concrete

Figure 30
Cheap cottages in Exhibition (now Nevells) Road, Letchworth, 1905. 'The Stone House' at left was designed by Bennett and Bidwell.
[© First Garden City Heritage Museum]

Figure 31
'The Nook', No 2 Cross Street: 1905 exhibit designed by Clare and Ross, now sensitively restored and extended.
[DP088812]

Figure 32
No 158 Wilbury Road: 1905 exhibit designed by John
Alexander Brodie, city engineer of Liverpool, in a radical
heavy concrete panel system.
[© First Garden City Heritage Museum]

cottage, was built with blocks made on site. No 212 Nevells Road, 'The Stone House', by Bennett and Bidwell, used textured artificial stone blocks. On Wilbury Road were two revolutionary concrete cottages: No 140, 'The Round House', was a rationalised concrete panel construction by Hesketh and Stokes for Cubitts (demolished 1987); No 158 (Fig 32), another pioneer of panel prefabrication, was designed by John Alexander Brodie (1858–1934), city engineer of Liverpool, who had designed a system that had been used for that city's tenement blocks (now demolished) – happily its radical exterior, with a hint of Art Nouveau elegance, survives to grace the Grade II* listing, conferred in 1979.

Nos 150–6 (even) Wilbury Road – mansard-roofed cottages by Arthur Hugh Clough of Burley, Ringwood, Hampshire – were possibly supervised by his nephew, (Sir Bertram) Clough Williams-Ellis (1883–1978). Finally, No 126, an almost puritanically simple cottage designed by Arthur Randall Wells (1877–1942), was a prizewinner. First Garden City Ltd's two gabled terraces of 'ploughmen's cottages' in Paddock Close, designed by the Hitchin architect, Geoffry Lucas, won the prize in the grouped category. A small estate of mansard-roofed houses on Birds Hill was affectionately known as 'Noah's Ark Cottages'. The 1907 Urban Cottages Exhibition, again at Letchworth, provided a demonstration of town planning, so grouped schemes predominated. Courtenay Melville Crickmer won several prizes, Nos 7–17 (odd) Lytton Avenue (Fig 33) being a fine example, with its roughcast walls, tile-hung

Figure 33
Nos 7–17 (odd) Lytton Avenue (originally Middle Street):
prizewinning cottages designed by Courtenay Melville
Crickmer for the 1907 Urban Cottages Exhibition.
[DP088436]

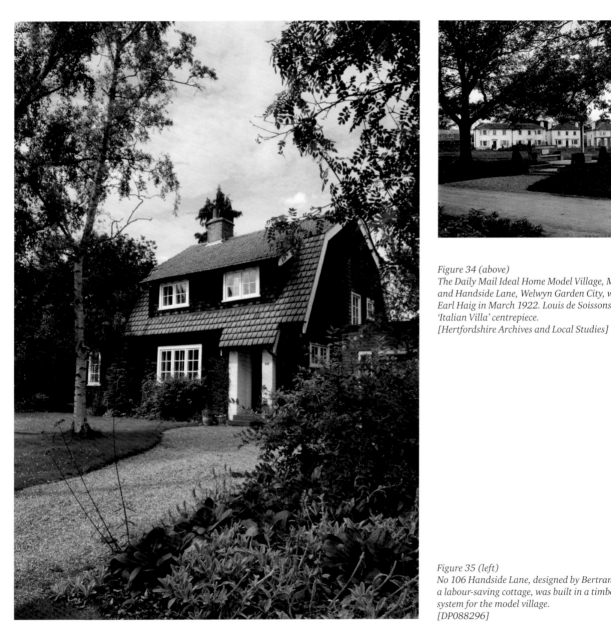

Figure 34 (above)
The Daily Mail Ideal Home Model Village, Meadow Green and Handside Lane, Welwyn Garden City, was opened by Earl Haig in March 1922. Louis de Soissons designed the 'Italian Villa' centrepiece.
[Hertfordshire Archives and Local Studies]

Figure 35 (left)
No 106 Handside Lane, designed by Bertram Parkes as a labour-saving cottage, was built in a timber-framed system for the model village.
[DP088296]

Figure 36
This imposing pair of exhibits, Nos 102 and 104 Handside Lane, was designed by Theodore Leake and built by disabled ex-servicemen trained by the Ministry of Labour. [Hertfordshire Archives and Local Studies]

jettied gables and mansard-roofed ends. The exhibition also included model smallholdings, spaced out along the Baldock Road.

The Daily Mail Ideal Home Model Village, built at Welwyn Garden City in 1921, provided another public event in the promotion of good housing design (Fig 34). Forty-one houses (of which 19 had been commissioned by Second Garden City Ltd) were built at Meadow Green and Handside Lane, and opened by Earl Haig in March 1922. Louis de Soissons designed a flat-roofed, rather Italianate, centrepiece built in concrete and later extended and converted to flats. Other entries featured steel framing and sand lime bricks. No 106 Handside Lane (Fig 35) was based on a Canadian timber-framed system and clad in timber shingles, with a Dutch-tiled gambrel roof enveloping the first floor. Next door, Nos 102 and 104 (Fig 36) were an imposing Lutyensian semi-detached pair, built in solid red brick by disabled ex-servicemen, trained under the Ministry of Labour.

Home and hearth

The three pioneer garden city settlements illustrate common features in their architecture, but also developments in style. In Letchworth (Fig 37), informal Arts and Crafts designs predominated until the 1920s, but in Hampstead Garden Suburb the influence of Lutyens spread Queen Anne and neo-Georgian designs from about 1910. Apart from the earliest council housing built in Handside Lane in 1920–1, Welwyn Garden City largely adopted neo-Georgian from the outset, implemented with finesse and ingenuity by de Soissons.

The presiding geniuses at Letchworth were Barry Parker and Raymond Unwin: their numerous designs set the initial architectural agenda for the Garden City Movement. Their semi-detached houses in Letchworth Lane – 'Laneside' and 'Crabby Corner', both now 'Arunside' (Fig 38) – were built in 1904, in the vernacular tradition with white-painted roughcast walls, a prominent roof with picturesque groups of dormer windows, and tall chimneys. These created a norm, varied according to circumstances: more elaborate as 'The Coppice' (1905) or 'Glaed Hame', both Pasture Road (1906); minimalist in a house for Parker's craftsman brother, now 'Stanley Parker House', No 102 Wilbury Road (1909) (Fig 39), or 'Tree Tops', No 12 Cashio Lane (1910). 'The White Cottage', Croft Lane (1906) (Fig 40) revived

Figure 37 (below, left)
Spencer Gore (1878–1914) visited Letchworth in 1912. His painting Letchworth: The Road, *looking east along Wilbury Road, conveys the freshness of the infant Garden City.*
[Letchworth Museum and Art Gallery (North Hertfordshire Museum Service)]

Figure 38 (below)
'Laneside' and 'Crabby Corner' (both now 'Arunside'), Letchworth Lane, were designed in 1904 by Barry Parker and Raymond Unwin. 'Crabby Corner', shown here, was Parker's home from 1906 to 1935.
[© First Garden City Heritage Museum]

Figure 39
The simple life: Signe Parker in the house designed
in 1909 by her brother-in-law, Barry Parker, for her
craftsman husband, Stanley Parker. The interior was as
austere as the outside.
[© First Garden City Heritage Museum]

Figure 40
'The White Cottage', Croft Lane, by Barry Parker and
Raymond Unwin, 1906, revived the tradition of the
cottage ornée.
[DP088247]

a picturesque thatched cottage *ornée*. The grouped cottages of Westholm (1906), Birds Hill/Ridge Road (1906) and Pixmore (1907–9) (Figs 41, 42 and 43) were developed by Garden City Tenants (the local branch of the co-partners) – the last estate approached a neighbourhood unit in scale, with its own greens, recreation areas and Institute (now Hillshott School). In 1909–10 cost limits of £120 per dwelling influenced the design of terraced cottages in Common View (Nos 103–77 (odd) and 114–24 (even)) with colourwashed brick walls and casement windows, the upper floor largely contained within the interlocking tiled roofs. Taking the provision of social housing forward, the Howard Cottage Society was founded in 1911. Rushby Mead, their first scheme – begun under their predecessor, Letchworth Cottages and

Figure 41 (above, left)
Westholm Green, designed by Barry Parker and Raymond Unwin in 1906 for Garden City Tenants.
[DP088209a]

Figure 42 (top)
Aerial view, 2009, showing the cul-de-sac and green on Birds Hill, by Barry Parker and Raymond Unwin, 1906, for Garden City Tenants.
[NMR/26529/013]

Figure 43 (above)
Pix Road, the heart of a cottage neighbourhood, designed by Barry Parker and Raymond Unwin, 1906–9, for Garden City Tenants.
[© First Garden City Heritage Museum]

Buildings – was a landmark, with a sensitive site layout by Unwin and noteworthy contributions by Bennett and Bidwell, and Crickmer, both of which figured prominently in the design of council housing after the First World War.

Several of Parker and Unwin's former assistants made significant contributions at Letchworth. Bennett and Bidwell were influenced by M H Baillie Scott, and their notable houses included 'The Cottage', No 7 Willian Way (1909) – Bidwell's home (Figs 44 and 45) – which was gabled externally, with open-plan interior, robust joinery and cosy, hooded inglenook fireplaces. 'Carfax', No 501 Broadway (1909) was more elaborate. In their later houses along Broadway (1925) inter-war formality merged with late Arts and Crafts design. With its angled 'butterfly' plan, sturdy joinery and copper-hooded inglenook fireplaces, Bennett's home – 'Hall Barn', The Glade (1923) – displayed undiluted Arts and Crafts values. The practice also updated cottage design and layout at Jackman's Place (1919–21), a pioneer local authority scheme by the newly created Letchworth Urban District Council.

Figure 44 (below)
'The Cottage', No 7 Willian Way, Letchworth, 1909, by Wilson Bidwell for himself.
[DP088434]

Figure 45 (below, right)
Interior of 'The Cottage' in 2009, showing the original brass-hooded inglenook fireplace.
[DP088335]

Figure 46
'Three Gables', No 12 Croft Lane, Letchworth, 1907, by
Cecil Hignett for himself: photographed in 2009, the
house has been extended on the left.
[DP088260]

Cecil Hignett (1879–1960) had been an assistant in Parker and Unwin's Buxton office. In 1907 he designed 'Three Gables', No 12 Croft Lane (Fig 46), a thatched cottage for himself, which received wide publicity (he also worked on the design for Parker's studio). Aside from his important industrial work he designed many rather formal but distinctive inter-war houses, often with tri-partite subdivision of their front elevations – Nos 7, 9 and 11 South View (1924) are characteristic.

Crickmer was one of the most important garden city architects, making notable contributions to all three communities discussed in this chapter. He began with a pair of modest houses, Nos 15 and 17 Baldock Road, Letchworth (1904–5). 'Crossways', Hitchin Road (1906), one of his best early houses, was dominated by an 'M' gable with exposed vertical studding, a design simplified for 'Arana', Hitchin Road (1908), where the brick ground floor contrasted with the rendered first floor, creating a 'skirt and blouse' effect. His most elaborate house, with internal open planning, was 'Dean Row', Pasture Road, 1910–11

Figure 47
'Dean Row', Pasture Road, Letchworth, 1910 –11: one of Courtenay Melville Crickmer's finest houses.
[© First Garden City Heritage Museum]

Figure 48
No 29 Norton Way North: of six Letchworth houses by M H Baillie Scott, this remains the least altered.
[Mervyn Miller]

(Fig 47). Crickmer's best work included grouped houses and cottages. At the junction of Sollershott East and South View a dominant block was built in 1911: around the corner in South View, Nos 34 and 36 were a semi-detached assembly of two of his first prize cottages from the 1911 Gidea Park Competition, with distinctive narrow-gabled stair turrets forming a transition between single and two storey elements. Crickmer also designed for the Howard Cottage Society and extensively for Letchworth Urban District Council, with council housing in The Crescent and Pixmore Way (1919–21). In the late 1940s he was principal architect for the large Grange Council Estate on the north of Letchworth.

Baillie Scott was the most eminent architect to work at Letchworth. Between 1905 and 1908 he contributed five distinctive houses. 'Elmwood Cottages', Nos 7 and 7A, Norton Way North, were entered in the 1905 Cheap Cottage Exhibition: vernacular in character, framed by projecting gables, with an open-plan interior subdivided by the staircase. Dismissed from the competition for exceeding the specified cost (£420 for the pair against the £300 upper limit) they proved one of the most influential exhibits and were furnished by Heal's. Open planning is also found in No 29 Norton Way North, built in 1906 (Fig 48), a gem in which the front roof eaves is swept down to within three feet of the ground – this also occurs on the much larger 'Corrie Wood', Hitchin Road (1908). 'Spring Wood', Spring Road (1906) was altered and aggrandised by Hignett in 1929, but 'Tanglewood', No 17 Sollershott West (1907) has retained its radical 50ft open-plan living room. Letchworth is notable for its excellent pre-1914 houses and there are important examples by Charles Harrison Townsend (1851–1928), Halsey Ricardo, William Curtis Green (1875–1960), Lucas, Randell Wells and Harold Clapham Lander (1868–1955).

At Hampstead Garden Suburb, Unwin moved into Wyldes farmhouse in 1906 and opened his office in the handsome black-boarded barn alongside (which also accommodated the Hampstead Garden Suburb Trust for many years). For architectural consistency, Hampstead Garden Suburb was finer than Letchworth. Its location provided it with accessibility to central London, and the attraction of the adjacent Heath Extension gave it a cachet reflected in the Trust's ability to require high design standards throughout. However, its consistency did not stem from the influence of a single dominant architectural practice, for Parker and Unwin were joined by some of their best contemporaries and a range of styles was introduced.

Initially, Parker and Unwin's work in the suburb continued their Arts and Crafts idiom. The Hampstead Tenants' development of the Artisans' Quarter

Figure 49
Aerial view of the Artisans' Quarter, Hampstead Garden Suburb, 2009, looking east from Finchley Road.
[NMR/26445/036]

(Fig 49), behind the Finchley Road frontage at Temple Fortune, was Unwin's masterpiece of housing design, built between 1907 and 1909. Grouping of houses revived the traditions of English cottage building, updated through the Arts and Crafts Movement. Each frontage was a carefully designed ensemble, and road junctions were developed with key groupings and focal points, derived from Unwin's matured appreciation of the design theories of Camillo Sitte.

A walk around Asmuns Place, Hampstead Way (Fig 50), or Temple Fortune Hill, shows the variety, developed from simple designs, and their placing and spacing relative to the roadway. Nestled in the backland behind Hampstead Way was another significant Parker and Unwin building, 'The Orchard', a quadrangle of small flats designed for the elderly – a gabled brick structure with timber-clad gables and timber-framed balconies, opened by Henrietta Barnett in 1909. A pioneer of specialist social housing, the building was never modernised and fell into disrepair, to be demolished in 1970 despite protests by Sir Nikolaus Pevsner and the Victorian Society. North of the original Artisans' Quarter, Wordsworth Walk and Coleridge Walk were designed by Unwin's former assistant Arthur Herbert Welch (1883–1965) in 1910–11, while Addison Way (1911–12) showed Unwin's office at its best, particularly the hexagonal grouping around the junction with Hogarth Hill, emphasised with roadside hip-roofed turrets. Middle-class housing was developed around the fringes of the Heath Extension. Between Hampstead Way and the suburb boundary there was only a narrow swath of land, in which Unwin designed a cul-de-sac. Reynolds Close (1911) is a classic example of grouped and linked middle-class housing (Fig 51).

Heath Close, somewhat similar, holds a surprise at the end. There was a scarcity of accommodation for women of modest means – some employed in education and the civil service. Hence, Waterlow Court was built in 1909. The original residents took their meals in a communal dining hall. Approached through a timber-framed gateway, this quadrangle of housing, designed by Baillie Scott, recalls the calm of an Oxbridge college. Today Waterlow Court is owned by a residents' co-operative. Baillie Scott also designed the corner block running from Meadway to the south-east of Hampstead Way. Replete with genuine timber studwork, this is affectionately known as 'Baillie Scott Corner' (Fig 52). Behind, Linnell Close, by Michael Bunney (1873–1927) built in 1909–11, suggests a cathedral close in miniature with its substantial hip-roofed brick houses (Fig 53). Nearby in Linnell Drive is a gabled Cotswold-styled manor, built 1906–8 and designed by Sir Edward Guy Dawber (1851–1938) – one of an intended pair framing a vista, now lost, towards the Heath Extension.

Around 1910 the influence of Lutyens rippled out from the central squares subduing the prevailing vernacular character with elegant Queen Anne and neo-Georgian formality. No 27 Hampstead Way was meticulously designed in this vein by Welch, while next door, fronting Wellgarth Road, was a less assertive house in the same style, designed in 1910 – perhaps surprisingly

Figure 52 (above, left)
Genuine timber-framed construction on 'Baillie Scott Corner', 1909, at the junction of Hampstead Way and Meadway.
[Hampstead Garden Suburb Archive Trust]

Figure 53 (above)
Contrasting styles: Arts and Crafts (Michael Bunney) meets Edwin Lutyens lookalike (G Lister Sutcliffe) on Hampstead Way.
[Mervyn Miller]

Figure 55 (right)
Heathcroft Flats, by J B F Cowper, 1923, boldly faces the Heath Extension, with this spacious quadrangle behind.
[Hampstead Garden Suburb Trust]

Figure 54 (above)
The end pavilion on Corringham Road squares, 1912,
shows the influence of Edwin Lutyens on Barry Parker
and Raymond Unwin.
[DP088322]

– by Charles Cowles Voysey (1889–1991), son of C F A Voysey. Even Parker and Unwin caught the Lutyens influence in their Corringham Road squares (1911–12), where the chequerboard stone and brick pavilions are an inventive touch worthy of the master (Fig 54). After the First World War the Heathcroft Flats (Fig 55) on Hampstead Way (1923, by J B F Cowper) used Lutyens' 'Wrenaissance' style with panache. These were designed as 'labour saving', which involved compact planning for 'servantless' operation. Most of the 'New Suburb' was developed as a commercial venture by the co-partners and was thus contemporary with Welwyn Garden City: both adopted neo-Georgian as the dominant architectural style.

Crickmer made extensive contributions to Hampstead Garden Suburb architecture in a variety of styles. Some of his finest work is in the Arts and Crafts tradition. At the crossing of Willifield Way and the upper part of Temple Fortune Hill (1909) the blocks of housing frame a hexagonal space featuring his signature 'M' gables as eyecatchers (Fig 56). Aware of changing fashions, Crickmer worked with developers in the 'New Suburb' in the 1930s to create an iconic 'moderne' house type with streamform curved Crittall windows below a traditional tiled hipped roof – a house type used extensively, with a fine sequence in Howard Walk (1935).

Figure 56 (left)
'Crickmer Circus', 1909, with distinctive 'M' gables: part
of a fine group at the junction of Willifield Way and
Temple Fortune Hill, in Hampstead Garden Suburb.
[Mervyn Miller]

Figure 57 (above)
Welwyn Rural District Council housing, on Handside
Lane, designed by Courtenay Melville Crickmer in
1919–20, was among the earliest building in the new
garden city.
[Hertfordshire Archives and Local Studies]

Figure 58 (above, right)
Aerial view, 2009, showing the residential areas of
Welwyn Garden City developed in the 1920s.
[NMR/26434/021]

Crickmer also initially played a prominent role at Welwyn Garden City. Construction of the first 50 houses by Welwyn Rural District Council (the minor local authority within which the new garden city was located) began in 1919 along Handside Lane (Fig 57) – their painted roughcast walls resulted from a severe shortage of facing bricks. These strongly resembled Crickmer's contemporary local authority cottages in Pixmore Way, Letchworth. As de Soissons asserted his authority, more formal design predominated (Fig 58): for example, in Brockswood Lane, by C M Hennell and C H James; and Applecroft Road/Elm Gardens by de Soissons, where steep gambrel roof slopes were used for the upper floors to cut down on the expense of brickwork. In 1925 de Soissons designed concrete houses in Peartree Lane for the Welwyn Public Utility Society: here, long rationalist terraces were softened by trellised porches. Unfortunately, due to the clay subsoil, these suffered from cracking walls and were eventually redeveloped in the 1980s.

Supply and quality of local bricks – made by a company subsidiary – improved, and the mixed red facings proved an admirable medium for de Soissons' civilised early Georgian style, adopted for the majority of buildings. By the mid-1920s a virtuoso repertoire of grouped designs and street pictures emerged, for example The Quadrangle, off Valley Road (H Clapham Lander), Dellcott Close (Hennell and James) or Dognell Green, off High Oaks Road (de Soissons). Individual plots were let for imposing houses – one of the best, 'Badgers End' (Fig 59), towers like a sentinel over Brockswood Lane (Hennell and James). The area between Brockswood Lane and Guessens Road shows the inventive range of civilised neo-Georgian design, informally arranged as the contrasting counterpart of the formal axial planning of the town centre. Housing in the 1930s retained a minimalist Georgian aesthetic, as in the Woodhall neighbourhood in the south-east. The sweeping crescent of the Woodhall shops and the almost Scandinavian elegance of the community centre (Fig 60), with its pediment frontal supported on slender columns, created a centre with a real sense of place.

By the 1930s other styles were infiltrating the garden city communities, most noticeably in Hampstead Garden Suburb, where a spectacular 'moderne' cul-de-sac – Lytton Close, designed by G C Winbourne in 1935 (Fig 61)

Figure 59
'Badgers End', Brockswood Lane: an imposing house with 'sleeping porches', designed by C M Hennell and C H James in 1929.
[Hertfordshire Archives and Local Studies]

Figure 60
Woodhall Community Centre, Welwyn Garden City, 1938, by Louis de Soissons.
[DP088309]

Figure 61
Lytton Close in Hampstead Garden Suburb, 1935, by
G C Winbourne, liner architecture at its most seductive,
on a traditional cul-de-sac layout.
[DP088324]

– transposes a traditional grouping into white-walled, flat-roofed liner architecture, with streamlined windows and rooftop sun decks. The same year, at Belvedere Court on Lyttelton Road, Ernst Freud (son of Sigmund Freud) punctuated conventional blocks of flats with sweeping curvaceous pavilions, their windows organised into horizontal bands (Fig 62). Nor was Tudor Revival excluded, as manifested in an enclave around Edmunds Walk and Deansway (Fig 63), designed by R H Williams, enjoyable for picturesque silhouettes and high-quality reclaimed materials (while lamenting the sacrifice of the source of the plunder). More exotic was Cape Dutch – all white walls and coloured glazed pantiles – seen at Philip Hepworth's (1890–1963) 'Eliot House' (formerly 'White Walls'), No 40, The Bishop's Avenue (1924) (Fig 64), and Cowper's 'The Pantiles' flats on Finchley Road. More straight-laced under Parker's watchful eye, Letchworth cannot boast either exotica or moderne. However, in Hawthorns, off Pentley Park in Welwyn Garden City, Paul Mauger and Eugene Kent built some unassuming modernist houses in the late 1930s.

Figure 63
House in the 'Tudor enclave', Edmunds Walk, designed in
1935 by R H Williams.
[DP088327]

Figure 64
'Eliot House' (formerly 'White Walls'), The Bishop's
Avenue, Hampstead Garden Suburb, 1924, by Philip
Hepworth.
[DP088311]

4

Industry and commerce

Employment was a key feature of Ebenezer Howard's concept if the garden city was to become more than a dormitory town. It was essential to build a varied economic base as soon as possible. The innovative concept of industrial estates was pioneered at Trafford Park, Manchester, in the 1890s, and this provided the model for the planning of industrial zones within the garden cities, where they were sited to link easily with transport systems. Furthermore, industry was to have a new image in the garden city, where the polluted environment of the typical Victorian factory was to be replaced by spacious buildings, full of light, in contemporary style, and with better facilities for the workforce. Traditional heavy industry was deemed inappropriate: instead, the 20th-century industries were skill-based, adding value to imported raw materials. Craft-based trades, too, were seen as targets for attraction to the garden cities. Success depended upon availability of land, the infrastructure required by modern industry, and quality and quantity of labour. Planning could, and did, provide the first two. Both garden cities laid out generous industrial areas and provided some tenement or advance factories to attract smaller, promising companies. Larger concerns could acquire extensive plots with convenient access to rail and improving road transport. The labour issue was linked to providing adequate and affordable housing to attract skilled workers away from the established industrial centres. In all three factors, the garden cities were conspicuously successful.

At Letchworth, industrial development was led by Walter Gaunt, experienced as manager of Trafford Park. His mantra 'Factory sites to let' became a byword, satirised by artistically inclined middle-class pioneers, who felt that too much industrial development might harm their earthly paradise. But Gaunt chalked up some early successes, particularly the relocation of J M Dent, the publishers, from cramped inner-city London workshops. They built a large factory, which opened in 1907, and were soon printing their 'Everyman Edition', offering classic texts at modest prices. Dent even built advance housing for key workers – Temple Gardens, off Green Lane – which adapted London 'by-law' terraces. W H Smith brought their bookbinding workshop to Letchworth, with an impressive factory at the corner of Works Road and Pixmore Avenue. Engineering was another staple, including motor manufacturers, prior to automation of vehicle assembly. During the First World War, after the fall of Antwerp, Georges Kryn and Raoul Lahy arrived in

The meticulous restoration of Cecil Hignett's Spirella Building brought new life to an obsolete factory. [Letchworth Garden City Heritage Foundation]

Letchworth with pockets full of uncut diamonds and founded K & L Works, which produced armaments during the war (Fig 65), then turned successfully to heavy engineering.

The most famous industry of Letchworth was Spirella (Fig 66), who manufactured patent corsets stiffened by spiral wound springs. They opened temporary premises in 1910 and between 1912 and 1920 built their vast factory west of Bridge Road, designed by Cecil Hignett. A pioneer concrete-framed structure with Arts and Crafts touches such as the tiled pavilion roofs, it took pole position near the station rather than on the industrial estate. The factory had two glazed workshop wings, with a central block which included the canteen and a top floor ballroom in which gymnastic classes for employees were held. Spirella-trained sales ladies advanced across the nation, sending in their clients' measurements for bespoke garments. The company prospered until the 1950s and wound down until 1989, when only surgical corsets were manufactured. One of the most craft-oriented firms was Edmundsbury Weavers (Fig 67). Its founder Edmund Hunter moved to Letchworth in 1908,

Figure 65
Filling shells with explosives at K & L Works, Letchworth, 1915.
[© First Garden City Heritage Museum]

Figure 66 (above)
'Workers' Playtime': charabancs drawn up outside the Spirella factory, Letchworth, for the employees' outing to the 1924 British Empire Exhibition at Wembley.
[Letchworth Garden City Heritage Foundation]

Figure 67 (left)
Edmundsbury Weavers, Ridge Road, Letchworth, c 1909. Dorothea Hunter presides over a mainly female workforce.
[© First Garden City Heritage Museum]

Figure 68 (above)
The Shredded Wheat Factory and grain silo: a landmark of Welwyn Garden City, designed in 1924–5 by Louis de Soissons.
[Hertfordshire Archives and Local Studies]

Figure 69 (above, right)
Roche Products, Broadwater Road, Welwyn Garden City, 1938: an exemplar of continental modernism designed by Otto Salvisberg.
[Hertfordshire Archives and Local Studies]

and his factory in Birds Hill was designed by Barry Parker and Raymond Unwin. His wife Dorothea Hunter worked alongside him in the weaving shed. The firm was exceptional in paying its employees for two weeks holiday.

Welwyn Garden City built on the experience of Letchworth. The industrial zone was laid out on similar lines, with large plots, units of different sizes and good transport links, including private railway sidings. Industry developed quickly during the 1920s and produced some exceptional buildings expressing the modern nature of the industries attracted to the new city. The healthy image was boosted by the Shredded Wheat Company who built their factory fronting the railway in 1924–5 – an unusually modern design by Louis de Soissons, dominated by an enormous concrete grain silo (Fig 68). The original brand name 'Welgar' was derived from WELwyn GARden. Other key industries included Murphy Radio, by the 1940s one of the six largest electronic firms in the world. Pharmaceuticals became prominent when Roche Products transferred their United Kingdom operations to a site in Broadwater Road in 1938 (Fig 69). Their buildings, designed by Otto Rudolf Salvisberg (1882–1940), were the epitome of Swiss modernism. Their rivals, Smith Kline and French, developed their laboratories and offices – including the town's tallest building (Arup Associates, 1960–4) – at Mundells, to the north-east of the town centre, part of the later 'new town' expansion of Welwyn Garden City.

During the depression of the 1930s the garden city industrial estates were viewed as economic and social models as the Government sought to promote new industry in areas of high unemployment. Initiatives such as the Team Valley Trading Estate in Gateshead, built with public subsidy under the Special Areas (Development and Improvement) Act of 1934, drew their inspiration from the experience of the garden cities. The industrial estates were integral to Howard's vision of how industry could contribute to a new civilisation without compromising the environment.

However, the industrial upheavals of the late 20th century, as manufacturing outsourced to Asia, affected both garden cities. Letchworth lost Shelvoke and Drewry, specialist manufacturers of refuse vehicles since the 1920s; Borg Warner, manufacturers of automatic transmission for the motor industry; and International Computers, which had grown out of the British Tabulating Manufacturing Company, manufacturers of office equipment since the 1920s. At Welwyn, the Shredded Wheat Factory and the Roche buildings were empty by 2010, and Murphy Radio's showpiece factory of 1955 has long been demolished. Regeneration of obsolete industrial areas, long considered to be endemic in parts of the industrial north, was suddenly a feature of the two garden cities.

Both garden cities have always had their proportion of commuters to London. Those living in the south-west of Letchworth travelled from Hitchin Station, until the local service improved from the permanent station, opened in 1913. At Welwyn it was always accepted that many would make the daily grind to King's Cross. In the 1920s *Punch* pictured bowler-hatted commuters flinging their mud-encrusted Wellingtons from the carriage windows for the porters to sort out and stack neatly for the evening pick-up. However, at both garden cities there was a workforce commuting in from the surrounding villages where there were few employment opportunities. Commuting was, of course, the lifeline of Hampstead Garden Suburb, built in response to the construction of the Northern Line and its station at Golders Green. However, much of the suburb lay northwards, involving a mile-long tram ride down Finchley Road, or, from the 'New Suburb', a trek to East Finchley Station. The seemingly modest 'Tuppeny Tube' limited occupancy of the 'Artisans' Quarter' by those employed in manufacturing, for which there were few jobs nearby. Instead, white collar workers and those employed in clerical work or teaching found their homes here.

Figure 70
Hustle and bustle in Leys Avenue, one of the principal shopping streets in Letchworth, 1920.
[© First Garden City Heritage Museum]

Shopping was a vital link in the supply chain of both garden cities, situated in rural areas: even the few miles from Baldock or Hitchin posed problems for working-class residents in Letchworth before the First World War. The contrasted provision of shops between the two garden cities had repercussions for the form and status of their town centres, which remain evident today. Howard envisaged shops as a corporate responsibility, but lack of capital prevented this at Letchworth. Early development of working-class housing to the east of Norton Way resulted in construction of the first shops along Station Road and Leys Avenue (Fig 70 and *see* Fig 101) rather than Eastcheap (and Westcheap which was never implemented) following the master plan. Small general stores competed with each other until there was a critical mass of population. The imposing Co-operative store on Eastcheap fully opened in the 1920s – the only department store in town – by which time there were 162 commercial premises with such local stalwarts as Nott's Bakers, Moss's Groceries and Spinks' Drapers.

Figure 71
John Lewis (originally The Welwyn Stores), designed by
Louis de Soissons in 1939.
[DP088288]

Figure 72
Howardsgate, Welwyn Garden City, begun 1929. In addition to the buildings, Louis de Soissons also designed the lamppost and poster display unit.
[DP088303]

At Welwyn Garden City the company established a retail subsidiary which held a monopoly for a decade. The Welwyn Stores (Fig 71) were initially under Charles Benjamin Purdom's management: he had worked in the Letchworth Estate Office and attained a position of power at Welwyn. From today's perspective, his critique of financial procedures appears to resemble creative accounting. In temporary premises, the stores were a department store in miniature, with a bookshop and lending library in addition to the expected food, clothing, hardware and furniture. Contemporary photographs show a cluttered Aladdin's cave. Despite residents' criticism, marketing surveys claimed that prices were competitive with St Albans and Hertford. However, the stores had enabled the infant garden city to enjoy a fuller range of goods and services in its earliest years, and in June 1939 its imposing new premises opened. These faced The Campus, east of Parkway, and where designed by de Soissons in simplified Georgian style with a central pediment. The town centre began to build up as new shops were allowed. The first was W H Smith on Howardsgate in 1930 (they had opened in Letchworth in 1907), on the corner of a parade from the Midland Bank. The first bank, Barclays, had opened in 1922, in a timber hut: its landmark permanent building, also designed by de Soissons, set the tone for Howardsgate in 1929 (Fig 72).

Hampstead Garden Suburb relied on the Finchley Road and Golders Green shops. Unwin's 1905 plan had included two shopping parades in his 'village' centre, which somehow got lost in the transition to Edwin Lutyens' grand central squares. The two imposing blocks forming the suburb gateway at Temple Fortune had ground-floor shops with spacious flats above, approached by an access deck, above a sunken delivery area – a remarkably progressive arrangement. The relative isolation of the 'New Suburb' resulted in development of The Market Place in the 1930s astride the Falloden Way/ Lyttelton Road diversion of the A1. Traffic cumulatively undermined its appeal, particularly to passing trade. The area's upper income residents had increasing access to alternative centres, and as a result shopping provision in and for the suburb never seems to have quite gelled.

5

The Spirit of the Place

Garden city lifestyle quickly became identified with liberal movements and cult religions of the early 20th century. Letchworth became notorious nationwide for its unconventional citizens, promenading around their Utopia in smocks and sandals, womenfolk resplendent in flowing robes, hatless and gloveless. Free-thinking, middle-class reformists, albeit a minority, took up abode in 'The village named Morality' (a name coined by John Buchan (1875–1940), who sent his derring-do hero, Richard Hannay, to seek out fifth columnists and pacifists in the garden city of 'Biggleswick', an entertaining episode in his novel *Mr. Standfast*).[15] Pacifism, internationalism, vegetarianism, temperance, Esperanto and theosophy had their niches in garden city life. Old-time festivities were revived for May Day (Fig 73); there were Arbor Days to celebrate tree-planting. Londoners flocked to visit the human zoo on Bank Holidays, an outing popularised by the Cheap Cottage Exhibition in 1905, and satirised in a famous local cartoon of 'What some people think of us' in 1909 (Fig 74).

Now a part of the Henrietta Barnett School, the Hampstead Garden Suburb Institute combined high community ideals with Edwin Lutyens' imitable design values.
[DP088316]

Figure 73 (right)
May Day in Howard Park, Letchworth c 1912.
[© First Garden City Heritage Museum]

Ebenezer Howard's first wife died in 1904 and a subscription was raised to build the Mrs Howard Memorial Hall (1905), a neat Barry Parker and Raymond Unwin building on Norton Way South, in a sliver of meadowland later landscaped as Howard Park. Village hall size, the hall was a major cultural centre accommodating plays, concerts, political debates and the garden city Pantomimes which poked gentle fun at the pioneer lifestyle, which many children also adopted (Fig 75). Co-author Percy Gossop, a leading light of thespianism, got up like a Burne-Jones Madonna, epitomised the Spirit of the Place, 'Genius Loci', and berated architects for their ever-so-draughty Arty Crafty cottages, to the tunes of Gilbert and Sullivan.

The equivalents in Hampstead Garden Suburb were annual summer pageants, held in the field behind the newly begun Institute, with the trees of Big Wood as an arboreal backdrop. Paul Jewitt's *The Masque of Fairthorpe*, performed in September 1910, cast the Nymph of the Mead and The Templar to repel Jerry Builder from the fields of Temple Fortune, where the Artisans' Quarter was under completion (Fig 76). In the wake of Jerry's retreat, a procession of architects, makers of regulations and governors arrived, and with almost Masonic fervour the chief architect (surely Unwin) commended the glorious task of providing 'stifled townsmen groping and gasping in their shapeless streets' with a glimpse of 'happy folk seen in a brighter hillside'.[16] The pageant *Adam Bell* was revived in June 1931, and the Duchess of York (later H M Queen Elizabeth the Queen Mother) joined the venerable Henrietta Barnett on the front row of the audience.

Home-grown entertainment was prevalent pre-1914, 'legitimate theatre' was an amateur preserve, and theatrical societies have long flourished in garden city communities. George Bernard Shaw's plays were popular, with an early performance in Letchworth of *The Showing Up of Blanco Posnet*, which had incurred the wrath of the Lord Chamberlain's censorship. At Welwyn Garden City in 1922, Sir Frederic Osborn parodied the play as *The Blowing up of Bolsho Poshnut*, a skit on local politics. Shaw's reaction (he lived nearby at Ayot St Lawrence) is not recorded. Charles Benjamin Purdom, whose theatrical alter ego emerged at Letchworth, pressed hard for a permanent theatre, which opened on Parkway in 1928 (Fig 77), but had by the early 1930s succumbed to the talkies – it survived into the 1980s as the Embassy Cinema. The modest Barn Theatre, off Handside Lane, has been a theatrical outpost for many years.

Figure 74
'What some people think of us', a 1909 cartoon by Louis Weirter, sends up the simple life and professional luminaries Walter Grant, Raymond Unwin and Howard Pearsall (1845–1919). [Mervyn Miller]

Cottages, Letchworth, from Recreation Field.
(Garden City Series.)

Figure 75 (above)
The young pioneers, Raymond Unwin's children, Edward and Peggy c 1906, wearing woollens, tweeds and handmade sandals, photographed in the field behind their Letchworth home shortly before they moved to Hampstead Garden Suburb.
[Mervyn Miller]

Figure 76 (above, right)
The Gardeners' Chorus of The Masque of Fairthorpe, *1910, assembles on the pageant ground, with the backdrop of Big Wood, Hampstead Garden Suburb.*
[Hampstead Garden Suburb Archive Trust]

The Letchworth Picture Palace on Eastcheap opened in 1909, was rebuilt in 1924, and demolished in the 1980s; the more modern Broadway Cinema opened in 1936 and has survived through rebuilding in 1995, which tripled the auditoria. Hampstead Garden Suburb avoided the cinema until 1930,

Figure 77
Parkway, Welwyn Garden City, c 1932, showing The Welwyn Theatre with Howardsgate in the distance.
[Hertfordshire Archives and Local Studies]

when a prime site on Finchley Road was developed for the mighty super-talkie Orpheum, downgraded and demolished in the early 1980s.

Howard's 'local option' of temperance was decided by referenda in Letchworth; every adult resident was enfranchised, when women's suffrage was far into the future. It is rumoured that the women's vote kept the town dry for many years. The Skittles Inn (now The Settlement), Nevells Road, was designed by Parker and Unwin in 1907 as an olde English inn, with skittle alley and bar counter but no alcohol (Fig 78). Mine host Bill Furmston had been one of the first pioneers to move from inner London. In a spirit of compromise, First Garden City Ltd allowed the public houses in Norton and Willian, hamlets on the edge of the garden city estate, to remain open, a long walk from working-class neighbourhoods. The Skittles Inn was reconstituted as an adult education centre, The Settlement, in 1923 and it still flourishes in this capacity. A similar atmosphere of earnest temperance hovered over Hampstead Garden Suburb: Henrietta Barnett promoted the Institute on Central Square for improving adult education (Fig 79). Its Edwin Lutyens building was enlarged piecemeal, also to accommodate the Henrietta Barnett School for Girls, which in 2007 ousted the Institute to new premises near East Finchley Station. The Club House, on

Figure 78 (left)
The Skittles Inn (now The Settlement), Letchworth, 1907, designed by Barry Parker and Raymond Unwin. The former skittle alley, now converted to a small theatre, is on the right.
[DP088252]

Figure 79 (right)
The opening of Queen Mary Hall at Hampstead Garden Suburb Institute, 1924. H M Queen Mary and Henrietta Barnett are clearly displeased at the state of the site.
[London Metropolitan Archives]

Figure 80
*The Club House, Willifield Green, Hampstead Garden
Suburb. Designed by Barry Parker and Raymond Unwin
in 1909: it fell victim to an aerial landmine in 1940.
[Reproduced by courtesy of the University Librarian
and Director, The John Rylands University Library, The
University of Manchester]*

Willifield Green, opened in 1909 (Fig 80). Strategically located between the Artisans' Quarter and the middle-class areas running up to Central Square, it was intended to foster mixing of the social classes. It was successful and hosted the 'Suburb Parliament' during the inter-war period: unfortunately, the Parker and Unwin building, with its landmark Teutonic watchtower, was victim to an aerial landmine in 1940. Second Garden City Ltd was less dogmatic and permitted a 'wet canteen' at The Cherry Tree in Bridge Road, Welwyn Garden City (Fig 81), housed in wooden huts, with an elegant trellised porch by Louis de Soissons. It was taken over by Whitbread in 1932, rebuilt and expanded. Further public houses followed in the neighbourhood centres of the post-war new town. In the early years, meeting rooms were huts – including a converted cart shed at Handside Farm and the Lawrence Hall in Applecroft Road.

Many garden city pioneers, sceptical of orthodox religions, sought alternatives. Theosophy, drawing inspiration from the identification of a new Messiah, a holy boy from India, was prevalent in Letchworth. Miss Hope-Rea contributed to the cost of building Vasanta Hall in Gernon Walk, an eccentric little building opened in 1914 by the leader of the movement, Annie Besant.

Figure 81
*The original Cherry Tree, Welwyn Garden City was
a surplus army hut, spruced up by Louis de Soissons'
elegant trelliswork.*
[Hertfordshire Archives and Local Studies]

Figure 82
The Cloisters, Barrington Road, Letchworth, 1906–7,
by W H Cowlishaw for Annie Jane Lawrence is now the
North Hertfordshire Masonic Centre.
[DP088242]

The architect was W H Cowlishaw (1869–1957): his masterpiece, The Cloisters (Fig 82), was built in Barrington Road on the rural fringe, in 1906–7, for Annie Jane Lawrence (1863–1953), an enthusiast for fringe religions. Intended as an open-air adult school, it owed much to Cowlishaw's interpretation of his client's dreams, and £20,000 had been spent when construction ceased in

Figure 83 (left)
'Howgills', South View, Letchworth, 1907, by Bennett and
Bidwell: this Friends' Meeting House was gifted by Miss
Juliet Reckitt of Hull.
[DP088253]

November 1907. The towering mass of grey brick, Purbeck stone, flintwork and orange tiling remains astounding, climaxing in an octagonal tower above the entrance. The flat roof had a balustraded walkway. The cloister garth was open to the south, accommodating acolytes of the Alpha Union in hammocks. A pipe organ serenaded the occupants, who began their day with a plunge in the unheated pool; meditation alternated with household tasks. The Society of Friends flourished in all three communities: 'Howgills', Letchworth (1907) (Fig 83), was funded by Miss Juliet Reckitt, daughter of the Hull industrialist George Reckitt, and the serene Bennett and Bidwell Meeting House was modelled upon 'Briggflatts', North Yorkshire. At Hampstead Garden Suburb, Fred Rowntree's (1860–1927) self-effacing meeting house lay below North Square, distancing itself from the pomp and circumstance of Lutyens' twin churches, St Jude's (Fig 84) and the Free Church, which dominated the centre of the suburb. Non-denominational Free Churches were also built at Letchworth (Parker and Unwin 1908, replaced in 1923 by the Classical red brick cross-plan building by Parker) and at Welwyn Garden City (the Dutch-gabled church of 1929 by de Soissons).

Figure 84
The distinctive silhouette of St Jude's, Central Square,
Hampstead Garden Suburb, was designed by Edwin
Lutyens in 1909.
[DP088318]

Figure 85
St George's, Norton Way North, Letchworth, with its landmark concrete flèche, 1964, by Peter Bosanquet of Brett, Boyd and Bosanquet.
[DP088213]

Figure 86
Church of Holy Family, Shoplands, Welwyn Garden City,
1967, by de Soissons, Peacock, Hodges and Robertson.
[DP088307]

Anglicans initially made do with 'chapels of ease' at Letchworth, but the 1960s churches of St Michael, Broadway Gardens (Laurence King, 1968), with its octagonal plan, and St George (Fig 85), Norton Way North (Peter Bosanquet of Brett, Boyd and Bosanquet, 1964), with its soaring concrete flèche – which internally forms the backdrop to the altar – are excellent examples of ecclesiastical modernism. At Welwyn Garden City, de Soissons appeared to be working outside his comfort zone on the mannered St Francis of Assisi (1935) with its truncated nave. The Roman Catholics built a charming temporary church at Letchworth in 1908 (now stripped down as the Church Hall): their permanent St Hugh's is a stolid light brick design by Dixon-Spain (1878–1955) of Nicholas and Dixon-Spain, of 1938 vintage but not built until 1962. Similar conservatism informed their first church in Welwyn Garden City, but the Church of Holy Family, Shoplands (de Soissons, Peacock, Hodges and Robertson, 1967), with its well detailed brickwork and tall campanile, makes a bold landmark in the 'new town' Digswell neighbourhood (Fig 86).

6

Tudor Walters, Wythenshawe and the new towns

In 1912 the Garden Cities and Town Planning Association (the Garden City Association's new incarnation following passage of the 1909 Housing and Town Planning Act) published *Nothing Gained by Overcrowding* by Raymond Unwin, which made a compelling case for lower-density, garden city-style housing built on lower-cost rural or suburban land. His diagrams – contrasting dense 'by-law' terraced housing and expensive hard paved streets and alleys with more open, wider frontage garden city housing, with communal allotment and recreation areas in the street block centres – were widely influential, and a handsome perspective view illustrated the benefits of *The Garden City Principle applied to Suburbs* (Fig 87).

The municipalisation of the garden city

In 1914 Unwin was appointed Chief Town Planning Inspector to the Local Government Board. However, in 1915 he was seconded to the Ministry of Munitions to plan and supervise munition workers' housing, including Gretna-Eastriggs in Solway, Scotland. Membership of the Tudor Walters Committee on Working-Class Housing followed: its report, published in 1918, adopted garden city housing standards for Government-subsidised local authority housing, enabled under the 1919 Housing Act. Unwin served the Ministry of Health as chief officer for housing and town planning until retirement in

Housing in the Panshanger neighbourhood of Welwyn Garden City by Oliver Carey built in the 1960s by the Commission for the New Towns, broke the traditional design mould of Louis de Soissons.
[DP088310]

Figure 87 (right)
The Garden City Principle applied to Suburbs: *Raymond Unwin's iconic diagram for regulated suburban expansion first appeared in 1912 in* Nothing Gained by Overcrowding.
[Unwin 1912 Diagram VII, 19]

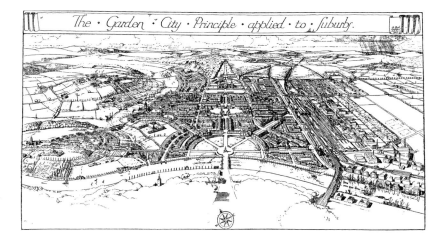

October 1928. In 1929 he was appointed technical adviser to the Greater London Regional Planning Committee. He played a leading role in monitoring the municipalisation of the garden city and moves towards regional programmes of new communities. Barry Parker too developed a leading role in design of council housing, and as consultant for the inter-war expansion of New Earswick. The new council estates on the fringes of English towns were not garden cities as envisaged by Ebenezer Howard, but they did represent a partial realisation of his vision for a new civilisation.

From parkland to Parkerland

One of the most complete municipal experiments in garden city design was carried out at Wythenshawe (Fig 88),[17] a few miles to the south of Manchester, a city bursting out of its boundaries by the early 20th century. Manchester's housing programme sprang from the enthusiasm of Alderman W D Jackson, chairman of the Public Health Committee, and E D Simon (1879–1960, created Baron Simon of Wythenshawe in 1947), chairman of the Housing Committee. In March 1920 Patrick Abercrombie identified Wythenshawe as the only undeveloped land suitable for building close to Manchester and recommended building a satellite, separated from the city by a green belt. That December the corporation resolved to negotiate purchase of the 2,468-acre (998.7ha) estate. Simon purchased the architecturally outstanding 16th-century Wythenshawe Hall and park, and presented them to the city. In October 1926 Unwin and W G Weeks held a public local inquiry into ministerial loan sanction for the projected satellite, which the Minister of Health, Neville Chamberlain, subsequently approved. In January 1927 the Corporation convened the Wythenshawe Estate Special Committee. The town clerk contacted Unwin, requesting advice about a consultant: Parker's appointment in August hinted at continued influence of the old partnership. Parker was urged to plan to combine amenity with financial advantage to the city.

    Lewis Mumford (1895–1990), the eminent American sociologist-planner, regarded Parker's plan as a bold updating of Howard's garden city. Parker had incorporated a variant on the Radburn neighbourhood superblock, recently designed by Henry Wright (1878–1939) and Clarence Stein (1883–1975).

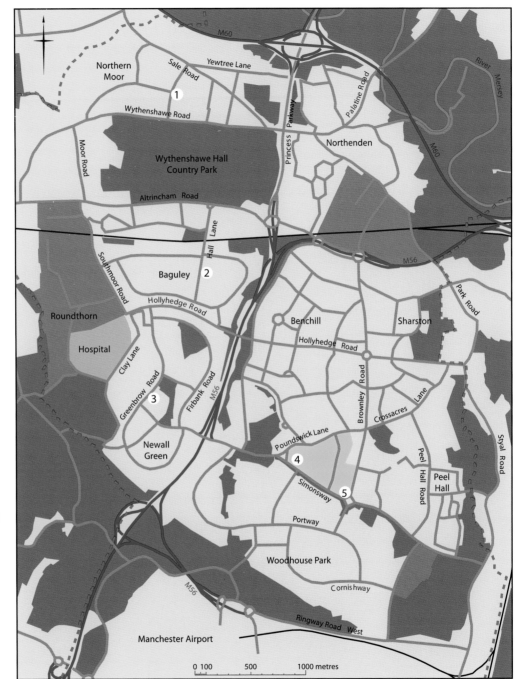

Figure 88
Map of Wythenshawe.

Key

1. St Michael's, Orton Road
2. Baguley Hall
3. St Francis's, Greenbrow Road
4. The Forum
5. William Temple Memorial
   Church, Simonsway

- - - - Manchester City
        Boundary

▬▬▬▬ Motorways

───── Railways

░░░░ Town Centre

▓▓▓▓ Industrial and
     Business

Parker's 1928 report specified a highway hierarchy of traffic streets and residential neighbourhood units with community facilities, a town centre, industrial zones, open spaces and a peripheral green belt. Most revolutionary were the main high-speed arteries, the parkways – attaining mature form in his 1931 plan (Fig 89) – reflecting his enthusiasm for American innovations and advanced practice.

Figure 89
Barry Parker's 1931 plan for Wythenshawe featured
sophisticated neighbourhood planning and landscaped
parkways, influenced by American practice.
[Macfadyen 1933 Fold Plan, 122]

Figure 90
Early development in Wythenshawe, 1931: mansard-roofed cottages designed by Barry Parker in liaison with Manchester City Council.
[Manchester Archives and Local Studies, Central Library]

Purchase of additional land by 1929 brought the landholding to 3,547 acres (1,435.4ha). Implementation was frustrated by hostility from the Cheshire rural districts, requiring private legislation to bring the land within Manchester's boundary. Economic depression in the 1930s and cutbacks in housing finance inhibited achievement of the full potential. Parker, 60 at the time of his appointment, continued as consultant until March 1941, but relations with the Manchester city architect, who designed most of the housing, became strained. Supported by Simon, Parker soldiered on. Notwithstanding the difficulties, Wythenshawe outstripped the combined population of Letchworth and Welwyn Garden City by the mid-1930s: testimony to the swift municipalisation of the garden city.

The layout retained Wythenshawe Park as a public amenity, with housing development to the north and south, including attractive mansard-roofed cottages (Fig 90). Parker's influence was to be found in the short culs-de-sac and articulated housing groups, similar to his designs in the western neighbourhood at New Earswick (Fig 91). Tree preservation was aided by

Figure 91
Barry Parker's cul-de-sac groupings at Wythenshawe were influenced by his contemporary inter-war work at New Earswick.
[Mervyn Miller]

Figure 92
Aerial view of the Benchill neighbourhood, Wythenshawe,
1937. The undeveloped land in the foreground was
reserved for extending the Princess Parkway, built as the
M56 in the 1970s.
[Manchester Archives and Local Studies, Central Library]

adjusting the layouts. The most intensive pre-war building occurred in the
Royal Oak, Benchill (Fig 92) and Sharston neighbourhoods, with an estimated
population of 21,000 by 1945 out of a total of 37,700. The most distinctive
buildings were churches: St Michael's and All Angels, Orton Road, Northenden
(Cachemaille-Day and Lander 1935–7) (Fig 93); the post-war St Francis's,
Greenbrow Road (Sir Basil Spence, 1959–61); and William Temple Memorial
Church, Simonsway (G G Pace, 1964–5). Neighbourhood shops were built
– for example the Sale Road 'Circle' – but the Second World War prevented
commencement of the major centre, which was relocated southwards in the
revised post-war layout and fitfully begun as an isolated precinct in 1962.
The *City of Manchester Plan 1945*, by R Nicholas, city engineer and surveyor,
anticipated a total population of 79,000 on completion in 1975 – the scale of a
'first generation' new town under the 1946 legislation. Indeed, Wythenshawe
was described as such in a City Council leaflet of 1953.

Figure 93 (above)
The remarkable concrete Deco-Gothic interior of St
Michael's and All Angels, Northenden, Wythenshawe,
1935–7, designed by Cachemaille-Day and Lander.
[Manchester Archives and Local Studies, Central Library]

Figure 94 (above, right)
Princess Parkway, Wythenshawe Road roundabout,
photographed July 1934, shortly after opening.
[Manchester Archives and Local Studies, Central Library]

The first section of Princess Parkway (Fig 94) was completed to Altrincham Road by 1933: its high-quality landscaping was sensational – striking confirmation that efficient function gave potential for beautifying form. However, it was always intended to continue south to Ringway, the new city airport (opened 1938) and beyond. The 1945 plan recognised that the parkway would become a barrier, dividing rather than unifying Wythenshawe. In 1969 upgrading to motorway standard began, sacrificing 50,000 shrubs and trees, and the route was renamed the M56, connecting Manchester and Cheshire, with the full system opening in 1974–5.

Housebuilding recommenced in the austere late 1940s, including corrugated steel-clad houses at Newall Green, known as 'Tin Town', and substantial, rather utilitarian dwellings at Baguley Hall, Crossacres, Woodhouse Park, Northern Moor and Brooklands – their standards prescribed under the 1949 Housing Manual. Later, the latter received the council's first high-rise blocks, Kingsgate, in 1957. There had always been a small proportion of private development, over which Parker exercised design control pre-war.

There were small private enclaves built in the 1950s and 1960s, but owner occupation in 1971 varied between 5–16 per cent – Northenden apart – compared to the Manchester average of 33 per cent. The blue-collar image lingered on for the remainder of the 20th century.

If Wythenshawe was the most comprehensive municipal undertaking on garden city principles, local authorities throughout England also implemented the standards in the new inter-war council housing estates. Some schemes were huge: Becontree, developed by the London County Council on the Essex outskirts of Greater London, housed over 100,000 people by 1934, 'a township more or less complete in itself'[18]; and the Watling and St Helier estates were other notable examples of the London County Council's municipal enterprise. Liverpool developed its Speke estate, Birmingham had Kingstanding, while Sea Mills, between Bristol city centre and Avonmouth docks, featured a layout derived from Unwin's iconic *The Garden City Principle applied to Suburbs* diagram. Others were small, perhaps only a few streets, but nevertheless proclaiming garden city design standards. A few company villages braved the harsher economic climate of the inter-war period: one of the most important examples being Silver End, Braintree, Essex, promoted by Francis Henry Crittall (1860–1935), manufacturer of mass-produced metal windows (Fig 95). Begun in 1926, the central buildings by C H B Quennell and earliest housing by C M Hennell, were traditional, but in 1929–30 the aesthetic spectacularly metamorphosed to moderne, designed by Thomas Smith Tait (1882–1954) and Frederick MacManus. It may seem ironic that, quantitatively, garden city ideas found their greatest expression in partial form in the expansion of old rather than in the creation of new settlements, but Howard would have approved of the great campaign to raise living and environmental standards in England's towns and cities.

Towards the new towns

Unwin's 1929 *Greater London Regional Planning Committee First Report*, the Marley Committee on Garden Cities and Satellite Towns (Report 1935) and the 1937 Barlow Royal Commission on the Distribution of the Industrial Population (Report 1940) all considered strategies for new settlements on a green belt background. Abercrombie, the most perceptive member of the

Figure 95
Silver Street, Silver End: housing by Frederick MacManus,
1927–8.
[k050172, © English Heritage Photo Library]

Barlow Commission, was appointed to prepare a County of London Plan (1943) followed by a *Greater London Plan 1944*, which converted the key principles of decentralisation, green belts and new towns into clear, practical proposals, and graphically illustrated a ring of new towns around London. In 1945 the incoming Labour Government, under Clement Atlee, appointed Lewis Silkin (1889–1972, created Baron Silkin of Dulwich 1950) as Minister for Town and Country Planning. He immediately convened a New Towns Committee under Lord Reith. The 1946 New Towns Act (together with the 1947 Town and Country Planning Act) created an all-embracing top-down planning system, with the development of new communities a state responsibility. A development corporation for each new town, financed by the Ministry, was responsible for master planning and implementation, with minor roles only for the elected authorities of the designated area. Amid heated local controversy, Stevenage, Hertfordshire, was designated as the first new town in November 1946.

Two months earlier a deputation from Welwyn Garden City, 16km south, met Silkin to urge its inclusion in the New Towns Programme. The company's plans for post-war expansion had proved controversial. In February 1947 Silkin intervened to limit growth and forbade northern expansion. That August, he announced his intention to designate Welwyn Garden City, together with the historic town of Hatfield, jointly as a new town. The designation order, made in January 1948, although hotly contested, was confirmed after a public inquiry. Louis de Soissons was appointed architect to the Development Corporation, ensuring continuity of planning and design: the official master plan appeared in 1949. The company was wound up on Government payment of £2.8 million for the assets.

The Development Corporation pursued a vigorous construction campaign. South-west and south-east neighbourhoods were completed. The north-west area was built between 1957 and 1964. Digswell Road was thrust northwards. The architectural tone was set by the Knightsfield Flats (Fig 96), elegantly Regency in style, with ironwork balconies. Designed by de Soissons in 1955, they were long regarded as an anachronism in the age of modernity. Wholesale modernism occurred in the 1960s and 1970s during development of Hatfield Hyde, Hallgrove and Panshanger – all extending the garden city eastwards. Daniells, designed by Oliver Carey in 1968, is an enclave of crisp modernist terraced houses, in the then fashionable light sand lime brick.

Figure 96
Knightsfield Flats, Welwyn Garden City, for New Town Development Corporation, 1955, by Louis de Soissons.
[DP088302]

In 1966 the Commission for the New Towns took over the assets of Welwyn and Hatfield for eventual disposal. The public housing was handed over to Welwyn Hatfield Council (the enlarged successor to the Urban District Council) in 1978, followed by town centre open spaces and Sherrards Wood in 1983: much local authority housing was sold to tenants under the 1980 Housing Act, 'Right to Buy'. The Commission retained the freeholds of the commercial buildings in the town centre and the industrial land. The former had continued in a traditional style until the 1980s, when plans for an enclosed shopping centre were revealed. Developed in partnership with British Rail, The Howard Centre absorbed the station, and its modernist concrete-and-glass pediment terminated Howardsgate. It opened in October 1990, a commercial magnet to counterbalance The Stores, which had been acquired by the John Lewis Partnership in 1983. Who knows what Howard might have thought? After all, he had proposed an enclosed shopping centre on his iconic diagrams. The Cherry Tree, the pioneer public house, was closed and redeveloped as a Waitrose supermarket in 1991: its bowling green is now a car park.

7

Conservation and the challenge of change

The grain silos of the former Shredded Wheat Factory at Welwyn Garden City pose a unique conservation challenge.
[DP088358]

A recent Government statement of policy, *PPS5: Planning for the Historic Environment* defines conservation as 'the process of maintaining and managing change to a heritage asset in a way that sustains and where appropriate enhances its significance'. The same publication defines a heritage asset as 'a building, monument, place, area or landscape positively identified as having a degree of significance meriting consideration on planning decisions'.[19] These may include designated assets such as ancient monuments, listed buildings and conservation areas, each of which categories confers a degree of statutory protection.

Individual buildings or ancient monuments can be listed or scheduled for their special architectural or historic interest. English Heritage estimates there are around 373,000 listed building entries – although these may include tombs or gravestones, not normally considered to be buildings – and list entries quite often include a group, which may comprise multiple individual units. Buildings are graded I, II*, or II, according to the degree of architectural or historic significance they possess. The top two grades, as they exist today, account for about 6 per cent of listed buildings: the remaining 94 per cent are Grade II. Alteration and extension to, and demolition of, listed buildings requires listed building consent, a procedure which is administered by local authorities – in consultation with English Heritage in appropriate cases. As well as individual buildings, places too can be designated for their special character and interest. Conservation areas were introduced in 1967, and there are now about 9,300. Identified for their 'special architectural or historic interest the character or appearance of which it is desirable to preserve or enhance', they are designated and generally administered by local authorities. They have been one of the great conservation success stories, helping to protect a range of settlements which include not only historic cities, towns and villages, but also many of the garden cities and suburbs with which this book is concerned. Proposals for designation of conservation areas have often stemmed from community concern, and there is a recognised pattern of consultation before local authorities take the formal decision to designate them. Afterwards, local authorities have a duty to prepare detailed character appraisals – for example, to identify buildings which positively contribute to the conservation area's distinctive architectural or historic character.

All of the communities discussed in this book have some listed buildings: some have many. The iconic twin churches designed by Edwin Lutyens in Central Square, Hampstead Garden Suburb are Grade I; the Spirella Factory at Letchworth Garden City is Grade II*; and the comparably individual Shredded Wheat Factory, at Welwyn Garden City is listed Grade II. At Port Sunlight virtually all of the distinctive, architecturally varied cottages are listed, together with more formal buildings such as the Lady Lever Art Gallery. The same situation prevails at Bournville. At Letchworth Garden City and Hampstead Garden Suburb much early housing, including working-class cottages, has been listed. By contrast, only a few buildings from the garden city era at Welwyn Garden City are listed: the Shredded Wheat and Roche factories and the elegant Knightsfield Flats, designed by Louis de Soissons in 1955, are all Grade II. Templewood School, Pentley Park (1949), one of Charles Herbert Aslin's (1893–1959) – the Hertfordshire county architect – finest prefabricated primary schools, is listed Grade II* (Fig 97). There has so far been no comprehensive listing study of the early garden city period.

At Wythenshawe major historic survivals are listed: Wythenshawe Hall (Grade II*) and Baguley Hall (Grade I). Listing of buildings from the garden suburb and post-war eras has been sporadic: the distinctive 1930s St Michael's and All Angels Church, Northenden (Grade II*) and the 1960s William Temple Memorial Church, Simonsway (Grade II) reflected the influence of specialist thematic studies, but the Jehovah's Witnesses Hall in Northenden owes its Grade II listing to its origin as the Forum Cinema of 1934. The Northenden Bus Garage, Grade II, evinced the technical virtuosity of its widespan concrete roof. Considering the generality of much of the housing at Welwyn Garden City and Wythenshawe raises the question as to whether comprehensive listing would be an appropriate way of preserving their distinctive garden city character, as much of this lies in the relationship between buildings, the road layout and the incorporation of green spaces and natural features.

Conservation areas have long existed in all of the major exemplars, with the exception of Wythenshawe, where only a small Victorian enclave in Northenden is designated. The definition of boundaries has had long-term consequences for the management of change to individual houses and the overall environment – for example, the conservation area at Welwyn Garden City is confined to the west of the railway, perhaps reinforcing the

Figure 97
Templewood School, Pentley Park, Welwyn Garden City, 1949, Charles Herbert Aslin, Hertfordshire county architect, project architect A W Cleeve Barr. [Hertfordshire Archives and Local Studies]

longstanding impression that the east was the wrong side of the track, although a small self-contained area in the Woodhall neighbourhood was later designated. Registration of important 'green enclaves' as historic parks or gardens is another means of recognising the distinctive ambiance of the garden cities. However, the registration of Broadway Gardens and Howard Park at Letchworth was not matched by equivalent status for Parkway and The Campus at Welwyn Garden City.

The responsible local authorities, North Hertfordshire District Council (Letchworth), Welwyn Hatfield District Council (Welwyn Garden City), Barnet London Borough Council (Hampstead Garden Suburb) and Manchester City Council (Wythenshawe) all provide a comprehensive range of conservation services. These include designation and review of conservation areas and preparation of development plans and local development framework policies to achieve the preservation or enhancement of their character or appearance. At Hampstead Garden Suburb, additional powers are provided by a detailed 'Article 4 Direction' (approved by the Secretary of State for the Environment in 1971 and subsequently strengthened), which controls householder work such as small extensions, replacement of windows or roof tiles. Detailed appraisals to identify the special factors – historic, architectural and environmental – which have shaped the local distinctiveness of these settlements have been undertaken at Letchworth and Welwyn Garden Cities, and have been circulated for community discussion before adoption as supplementary planning guidance.

Schemes of Management

In several of the communities discussed above, there is additional regulation outside planning legislation. This derived from the ground landlord powers of the original developers and was exercised through leasehold control. Originally, individual houses were not sold freehold but leasehold – typically 99 years at Letchworth and 999 years at Hampstead Garden Suburb and Welwyn Garden City. In 1967 the Government passed a Leasehold Reform Act enabling house owners to buy their freeholds, which nullified leasehold covenants. However, under Section 19 of the Act, the ground landlords could apply for a Scheme of Management (SoM) which would assist the overall preservation of 'well managed' estates. Approval by the High Court was required. There are interesting variants in the subsequent schemes and their governance. At Letchworth, the SoM is now administered by the Letchworth Garden City Heritage Foundation (LGCHF). The original developer, First Garden City Ltd, was taken over in the late 1950s, and Letchworth Urban

District Council promoted legislation to establish the Letchworth Garden City Corporation in 1963.[20] Under fresh legislation, its successor, the LGCHF, took over in 1995. At Hampstead Garden Suburb, the Trust was reorganised in the late 1960s, and also administers its SoM. At Welwyn Garden City, the original landlord powers were subsumed in the New Town Development Corporation and were passed to Welwyn Hatfield District Council by the Commission for the New Towns. Schemes of Management are also exercised through the Bournville Village Trust and the Port Sunlight Village Trust.

Examples of the work achieved under the SoMs include the publication of design guidance – jointly with the council planning authorities – for alterations and extensions of an appropriate scale, form and quality, and making grants to ensure the use of appropriate materials when houses are repaired. Letchworth Garden City Heritage Foundation recently commissioned a comprehensive building study to identify buildings of local architectural and historic merit, to monitor the extent of insensitive alterations and to assist the more effective use of renewed design guidance. A similar initiative has been undertaken in connection with surviving historic shopfronts in the town centre. Hampstead Garden Suburb Trust, in liaison with Barnet Local Borough Council, organised residents' groups within defined sub-areas to study and compile appraisals under the guidance of the Trust's architectural adviser, David Davidson, and was edited into a comprehensive document upon which future development control decisions would be based.[21] Barnet Borough Council completed consultation on the document during summer 2010 and it was adopted as supplementary planning guidance in the autumn.

These independent powers have sometimes been criticised by residents, some of whom see them as unwarranted extra layers of control over their ability to alter their properties. In the long-term, however, they have proved effective in conserving not only the overall quality of their settlements, but also in reining-in insensitive changes to individual houses. Hampstead Garden Suburb Trust has been notably effective at achieving this, and its active Residents' Association has generally been supportive. It might also be argued that good conservation has helped to increase the value of the properties, for character and authenticity are now cherished saleable commodities in the housing market.

Regeneration and the future of the garden city communities

However, conservation controls – whether administered by the local authority or a trust body – can only be a partial response to the perpetual pressure for change. A few years ago the Town and Country Planning Association (TCPA) studied the future of garden city communities, recording the ways in which key settlements had fared during the late 20th century and seeking ways of moderating change to achieve a benign outcome.[22] While all historic areas, many of them designated as conservation areas, are subject to change, garden city settlements are particularly vulnerable to loss of their essential character. Their importance lies in the integrity of the whole designed landscape, and insensitive change to one part – a poorly designed extension to a house, for example, or inappropriately scaled new building – can, therefore, damage a wider area. Front gardens and boundary features like hedges or fences are characteristic of these settlements, but the need for parking has placed them under great pressure. Furthermore, with their generous allowance of open space they appear to offer opportunities for additional housing, and they are therefore regarded by some as prime development sites. There is a clear danger that they will lose the precious features which make them attractive places to live and work.

The smaller, predominantly residential communities examined by the TCPA study appeared to be less susceptible to harmful change. Even so, the closing of the main Lever Factory at Port Sunlight, which is now used for Unilver's research and development arm, created problems of local unemployment and also controversy over the development potential of some of the surplus land. However, in the village centre there has been the opportunity to develop new social housing and a care home, integrated visually into the architectural ambiance of the surroundings. The Cottage Hospital has been regenerated as a boutique hotel, while the Girls' Club has become a state-of-the-art Heritage Centre (Fig 98). Bournville and Brentham are probably the least changed. The former is only a small part of a large tract of suburban land in south-west Birmingham developed and administered by the Village Trust, although the traffic generated by Cadbury World – a popular themed experience on the story of chocolate manufacturing – is an escalating problem.

Figure 98
The Heritage Centre, Port Sunlight (originally the Girls'
Club), 1913, by J Lomax Simpson.
[Mervyn Miller]

Brentham, in west London, is contained within contemporary suburban development and has few non-residential activities. It benefits from active residents' groups – the Brentham Society and Brentham Historical Society – which combined forces to produce an excellent centenary history of the suburb in 2001, published as a modern co-partnership venture.

Hampstead Garden Suburb has suffered since the 1920s from the traffic noise and severance of the controversial A1 link, cut through the north-east as part of the Barnet bypass. This has made regeneration of the Market Place as a neighbourhood shopping centre very difficult. On the Finchley Road, however, demolition of the Odeon (Orpheum) Cinema released land for Birnbeck Court, sheltered housing, with a landmark tower reminiscent of the old Club House on Willifield Green. Further south, a builders' merchant's yard was refurbished as a local Marks and Spencer store – a commercial anchor in the Finchley Road shopping strip. Most of the suburb's conservation problems seem to stem from extreme affluence: it is, for example, virtually impossible to create off-street parking for the myriad cars which line every road without the sacrifice of front gardens and the consequent loss of area character. There has been mounting pressure for demolition of existing houses, rippling across from The Bishop's Avenue, outside the Trust control area, but within the Hampstead Garden Suburb Conservation Area. While some of the original houses were not premier league architectural quality, their replacement 'Superhouses', which attempt, not always successfully, to incorporate overt characteristics of suburb architecture – inflated in size and inevitably including underground leisure suites – have cumulatively begun to erode the group harmony and generous spacing characteristic of the original garden suburb (Fig 99). Setback from Central Square, in 2010–11 the Henrietta Barnett School built low-key pavilion wings, designed by Hopkins Architects, as outriders to Lutyens' imposing (former) Institute.

Figure 99
'Suburban Superhouse', No 25 Winnington Road, Hampstead Garden Suburb, by William Bertram, 1998, David Landau Executive Architects.
[Hampstead Garden Suburb Trust]

The two garden cities, their original concept as self-sufficient settlements with a wide range of employment, leisure and shopping facilities, inevitably began to change in the post-war period. At Letchworth in the 1970s the old Commerce Avenue area was redeveloped as a precinct, now named Garden Square, which included a six-storey block of offices, leased to North Hertfordshire District Council, a multi-storey car park, and a public hall (long disused) above an indoor market (never successful and closed in 2009). The range of shops originally included two supermarkets, both of which soon became too small to survive. By the 1990s Sainsbury's had relocated to the business park on the fringe of Baldock. From 1995, the newly created Heritage Foundation promoted regeneration of buildings, including converting the locally renowned Broadway Cinema into a small multiplex. In the late 1990s the Spirella Building was refurbished without compromising its idiosyncratic character – even the cast-in concrete Arts and Crafts lettering advertising 'High Grade Corsets' has survived. The reincarnation of 'Castle Corset' as high specification offices (including the Foundation's headquarters) and a conference centre, is a notable success and a landmark in conservation, and was ceremonially reopened by the Prince of Wales in January 1999, with the 'Spirella ladies' in attendance.

The major regeneration effort in Letchworth was concentrated west of Broadway, where the North Hertfordshire College site was redeveloped with a Morrisons supermarket, accommodated behind the facades of several earlier buildings. New premises were also provided for the college overlooking Broadway Gardens (Fig 100), which was comprehensively relandscaped in 2003 to commemorate the centenary of the first garden city. More radical change occurred in 2009–10 through an £8 million wholesale 'street scene' redesign of the key shopping streets, Eastcheap and Leys Avenue by LDA Design, with high-quality materials and a pedestrian-friendly environment, which was completed in June 2010 (Fig 101 and *see* Fig 70). A striking feature is the sculptural group by Mel Chantrey – three vertical forms in bronze, invoking the torch of the garden city handed down to future generations. This regeneration *is* seen as a prelude to two comprehensive schemes to upgrade the town's status as a commercial centre. The Wynd, behind Leys Avenue and Station Road, is to be redeveloped with mixed retail and residential uses. Planning permission was granted in summer 2008 and purchase of the

individual sites is proceeding. A second phase, involving the 1950s Arena
Parade, between Eastcheap and Broadway, is likely to follow.

Welwyn Garden City had already faced up to far-reaching change as a first
generation new town, as recounted in Chapter 6. The Howard Centre, along
the railway perimeter, took the last major opportunity site, and the town centre
is now tightly constrained between the railway, The Campus and Parkway –
the latter two being among its most characteristic green vistas. There is some
possibility of development south of Howardsgate, but this is limited by the
presence of the Free Church, although Sainsbury's commenced rebuilding their
premises in Church Road in summer 2010. Developers have, therefore looked
to the industrial land immediately east of the railway. This area contains two
of the most iconic inter-war factories – Shredded Wheat and Roche Products

Figure 100
Aerial view of relandscaped Broadway Gardens,
Letchworth, 2003, photographed 2009, showing the new
North Hertfordshire College and Morrisons supermarket,
top left.
[NMR/26529/021]

Figure 101
'Street scene' improvements in Leys Avenue, Letchworth, by Letchworth Garden City Heritage Foundation, 2009–10. The symbolic sculptures by Mel Chantrey, frame the sweeping view down Leys Avenue.
[Letchworth Garden City Heritage Foundation]

– both now listed. Much of the land between the railway and Broadwater Road had been cleared and both factories stood empty by spring 2009. The council's consultants, Urban Practitioners, prepared a brief and master plan, which included housing, mixed-use development and a community centre, forming a comprehensive central neighbourhood. Quite how the listed grain silo of the Shredded Wheat Factory can be preserved or reused is an intriguing and possibly intractable conservation problem. Proximity to the town centre and split ownership between commercial rivals has complicated matters. Refusal of housing development and the proposed conversion of the Roche building to a church were considered on appeal in February 2010: the inspector subsequently dismissed the appeal solely on the ground of insufficient affordable housing and found the design matters and impact on the listed Roche building acceptable. Implementation would regenerate an area of dereliction close to the town centre and could act as a stimulus to bringing forward redevelopment of the remainder of the Broadwater Road West area. Although outside the conservation area, this land is within the original garden city as it was conceived in 1920, and recognition of this in both the form and use of the site will require constructive engagement of all parties. It highlights the pressure for change in a community which besides being a garden city is also now an economic hotspot of the south-east.

The initial development of Wythenshawe was contemporary with Welwyn Garden City, and it shared many of the same visual characteristics. Those apart, its social and economic indicators could not be more different. The TCPA study found that it fell short of achieving the comprehensive development that Parker had pressed for and became little more than a satellite estate, with poor connections to Manchester city centre and also to nearby towns such as Sale and Altrincham. Moreover, the upgrading to motorway status of Parker's Princess Parkway caused an irreparable fissure in the fabric of the estate. Further dislocation resulted from the resiting of the proposed town centre southwards after the Second World War – this had the effect of cutting it off from much of the north of the estate. The new centre was implemented as a pedestrian precinct comparable with the first generation new towns.

The population of Wythenshawe declined from 72,063 in 1991 to 66,267 in 2001, but subsequently began to increase, partially as a result of new housing construction. Social problems are legion. The proportion of single male adult households and lone parents with dependent children has increased. Fewer Wythenshawe residents are employed than the regional average, despite the presence nearby of major employers such as Manchester Airport. Almost half of Wythenshawe falls within the poorest communities in England. This formidable challenge was evident from comments made at the round table meeting, held during the TCPA study. What was equally striking, however, was that notwithstanding physical deterioration and visually insensitive alterations, Wythenshawe retains its inter-war garden city design characteristics, and is branded by the city council as 'Manchester's Garden City'. Much of the housing has been devolved to two major Registered Social Landlords – Parkway Green (West Wythenshawe) and Willow Park (east of Princess Parkway/M56) – who have pursued substantial regeneration and new build programmes, albeit that the latter incorporate few garden city design characteristics. This may be a missed opportunity, although the scale of their programmes is impressive.

The town centre has been significantly improved, with a £19 million redevelopment of The Forum, which incorporates a sports centre, swimming pool, library and community drop-in centre. Further phases included childcare and healthcare centres, creating a critical mass of leisure, cultural and healthcare facilities completed in 2006. The town centre master plan has been updated to attract further retail and office development and a new bus station.

In 2004 the city council launched the Wythenshawe Strategic Regeneration Framework (SRF) to promote comprehensive and coordinated investment for physical and social improvement over a 10 to 15-year period: to date over £600 million has been spent. The SRF defined a horseshoe of development and employment opportunities, with Manchester Airport at the south end and in the centre the traditional heart of the estate, with social infrastructure in a series of neighbourhood centres, which would be the key to local commitment to social regeneration. Amongst the 12 key objectives was making Wythenshawe a more attractive place to live and work by managing and improving its natural assets, parks and open spaces, leafy streets and mature landscape – the verdant background which has always been at the heart of true garden city community plans. A planned Metrolink tramway extension is proposed to run through the area connecting the neighbourhoods to the airport and to the city centre. The framework was a bold strategic move, different in scale and character to the development plans for the other garden city settlements, and is geared to updating the city's development plan. Local plans, generated at neighbourhood level, with community participation and agency partnerships, are under preparation. The West Wythenshawe Local Plan includes the early Baguley (Fig 102) and Royal Oak neighbourhoods, Wythenshawe Hospital, Roundthorn Industrial Estate, Oaks Business Park and Brookway Retail Park: the plan completed consultation in summer 2008. A plan for Northenden on the north-east is now being prepared. Already a new riverside park has proved a popular focus for community involvement. A 'real lives' initiative recruits local residents as 'ambassadors' in a campaign to challenge negative attitudes about Wythenshawe. If it can also connect to wider appreciation of Wythenshawe's garden city heritage, it may prove a key to success.

Figure 102
Blossom time in Baguley, Wythenshawe, in 2008 affirms its garden city credentials, with abundant tree-planting and woodland preservation.
[Wythenshawe Partnership Office]

Conclusion

All garden city settlements, both those discussed in this book and many others as well, have special interest in the way that they demonstrate, to a greater or lesser degree, Ebenezer Howard's vision of a new civilisation (Figs 103 and 104). It is easy now to forget just how radical his ideas were, for many of them became the orthodoxy of the middle decades of the 20th century and influenced post-war planning in new towns. Not all garden city settlements are protected by national or local schemes of designation, but this does not mean they are lacking in value. The fact that, despite some constraints, they remain highly desirable places to live demonstrates they are still widely recognised

Figure 103
Landing in New York in 1925 for the International
Garden Cities and Town Planning Federation Conference:
(left to right) Ebenezer Howard, Barry Parker and
Raymond Unwin.
[RIBA Library Photographs Collection, RIBA53086]

Figure 104
Ebenezer Howard memorial plaque by James Woodward,
Howardsgate, Welwyn Garden City.
[DP088363]

as having qualities not present in other sorts of urban environment. However, the pressures are undeniable and remorseless. The challenge is to find a way of adapting garden city settlements to modern living while retaining their character and identity. Success will ultimately depend on a number of things. Designation provides an assessment of significance and a degree of control over development. Through strategic planning, Government and local authorities are able to formulate policies which encourage sensitive management and provide guidance on how change – both large and small – can be designed to enhance rather than detract from special character. Perhaps most important, however, are the attitudes and actions of individual householders and communities and their degree of ownership of shared community values. The most powerful tools in the search for solutions will be the recognition of how their part in these unique environments is significant along with their appreciation and enjoyment of the character of the garden city communities.

Notes

1 Howard 2004, 28

2 G B Shaw letter to A C Howard (Howard's son), 25 May 1928, *see* Beevers 1988, 181

3 Notes by Ebenezer Howard, *see* Macfadyen 1933, 20

4 Quotation from *Sesame and the Lilies*, cited by Howard 1946, 50

5 *See* Hubbard and Shippobottom 1988

6 *See* Harrison 1999

7 *See* Reid 2001

8 For the early history of the Association, *see* Hardy 1991, Beevers 1988 and Macfadyen 1933

9 For the early history of New Earswick, *see* Joseph Rowntree Village Trust 1954

10 The published Building Regulations were reprinted in Purdom 1913, Appendix K: a classic account of the first decade of development at Letchworth. Unwin also wrote counterpart Regulations for Hampstead Garden Suburb.

11 For a modern biography, *see* Creedon 2006. For her own account, *see* Barnett 1928.

12 *See* Hampstead Garden Suburb 1907, 18. Strangely, Mrs Barnett did not quote these remarks in her later detailed account of the foundation ceremony (*see* Barnett 1928, 8–13).

13 The initial use of his oft-quoted verdict was on the occasion of the Golden Jubilee of Hampstead Garden Suburb in 1957, *see* Pevsner 1957, 43–5. Pevsner also wrote of Hampstead Garden Suburb in Cherry and Pevsner 1998, 139.

14 Publicity of the 1905 event was extensive. *The Book of the Cheap Cottages Exhibition* was an illustrated catalogue of the exhibits which included plans and summary specifications. The contemporary architectural and technical press included many articles. The subsequent 1907 Urban Cottages Exhibition was commemorated by an attractive guide to Letchworth, *Where Shall I Live*, published by First Garden City Ltd in 1907.

15 John Buchan convalesced at 'Derenda Cottage' (now 'Rest Harrow'), Willian Way, owned by a Captain Trotter, in 1915 before returning to serve in France. The Letchworth Fellowship of International Goodwill had held meetings with speakers from the British 'Stop the War' campaign, which provided Buchan with his raw material, Johnson 1976, 76.

16 *The Masque of Fairthorpe as first set forth at the Hampstead Garden Suburb, Saturday 10 September MDCCCCX*, written and contrived by E Paul Jewitt and first set forth by friends and neighbours, printed at the Garden City Press Ltd, Letchworth.

17 The early history of planning Wythenshawe is summarised in Miller 1992, 183–4. The most comprehensive published account, Deakin 1989, is stronger on local and social history. The ambitious post-1945 plans are summarised in Nicholas 1945.

18 *See* Home 1997, 7

19 *See* Department for Communities and Local Government 2010, 13

20 There are two detailed accounts of this remarkable achievement: Plinston 1981 and Purdom 1963.

21 Blackburn 2009, 35–6

22 The project ran from 2004–8. The author was an adviser on the Steering Committee. *See* Town and Country Planning Association 2008.

References and further reading

Barnett, H 1928 *The Story of the Growth of the Hampstead Garden Suburb, 1907–1928*. London: Hampstead Garden Suburb Trust (facsim edn Hampstead Garden Suburb Archive Trust 2006)

Beattie, S 1980 *A Revolution in London Housing*. London: Architectural Press in association with the Greater London Council

Beevers, R 1988 *The Garden City Utopia: A Critical Biography of Ebenezer Howard*. London: Macmillan

Blackburn, J 2009 'Hampstead Garden Suburb: A Novel Approach to Character Appraisal'. *Conservation Bulletin* **62**, August 2009, 35–6. *See* http://www.english-heritage.org.uk/publications/conservation-bulletin-62/ (accessed 4 October 2010)

Cheap Cottages Exhibition 1905 *The Book of the Cheap Cottages Exhibition* London: County Gentleman and Land and Water

Cherry, B and Pevsner, N 1998 *London 4. North*. London: Penguin (originally published as two volumes by Pevsner, N: *Middlesex* 1951 and *London, except the cities of London and Westminster* 1952)

Creedon, A 2006 *Only a Woman: Henrietta Barnett – Social Reformer and Founder of Hampstead Garden Suburb*. Chichester: Phillimore

Creese, W L 1966 *The Search for Environment: The Garden City Before and After*. New Haven and London: Yale University Press

Darley, G 1975 *Villages of Vision*. London: Architectural Press

Deakin, D (ed) 1989 *Wythenshawe: The Story of a Garden City*. Chichester: Phillimore

Department for Communities and Local Government 2010 *Planning Policy Statement 5: Planning for the Historic Environment*. *See* http://www.communities.gov.uk/publications/planningandbuilding/pps5 (accessed 4 October 2010)

Department for Communities and Local Government, Department for Culture, Media and Sport and English Heritage 2010 *PPS5 Planning for the Historic Environment: Historic Environment Planning Practice Guide*. *See* http://www.english-heritage.org.uk/publications/pps-practice-guide (accessed 4 October 2010)

de Soissons, M 1988 *Welwyn Garden City: A Town Designed for Healthy Living*. Cambridge: Publications for Companies

First Garden City Heritage Museum, www.gardencitymuseum.org (accessed 4 October 2010)

Hampstead Garden Suburb 1907 *Cottages with Gardens for Londoners*. London: Hampstead Garden Suburb Tenants Ltd (Hampstead Garden Suburb Archive Trust, S Box 8)

Hardy, D 1991 *From Garden Cities to New Towns. Campaigning for Town and Country Planning 1899–1946*. London: Spon

Harrison, M 1999 *Bournville. Model Village to Garden Suburb*. Chichester: Phillimore

Home, R 1997 *A Township Complete in Itself: A Planning History of the Becontree/Dagenham Estate*. London: Libraries Department, London Borough of Barking & Dagenham and School of Surveying, University of East London

Howard, E 1946 *Garden Cities of Tomorrow* (edited with preface by F J Osborn). London: Faber and Faber (originally published in 1902 as *Garden Cities of Tomorrow*. London: Swann Sonnenschein)

Howard, E 2004 *Tomorrow: A Peaceful Path to Real Reform* (with commentary by Hall, P, Hardy, D and Ward, C). London: Routledge (originally published in 1898 as *Tomorrow*. London: Swann Sonnenschein)

Hubbard, E and Shippobottom, M 1988 *A Guide to Port Sunlight Village*. Liverpool: Liverpool University Press

Johnson, K 1976 *The Book of Letchworth: An Illustrated Record*. Chesham: Barracuda

Joseph Rowntree Village Trust (Waddilove L E) 1954 *One Man's Vision: The Story of the Joseph Rowntree Village Trust*. London: George Allen and Unwin

Macfadyen, D 1933 *Sir Ebenezer Howard and the Town Planning Movement*. Manchester: Manchester University Press

Miller, M 1992 *Raymond Unwin: Garden Cities and Town Planning*. Leicester: Leicester University Press

Miller, M 2002 *Letchworth: The First Garden City*. Chichester: Phillimore (first published in 1989)

Miller, M 2006 *Hampstead Garden Suburb. Arts and Crafts Utopia?*. Chichester: Phillimore

Nettlefold, J S 1908 *Practical Housing*. Letchworth: Garden City Press

Nicholas, R 1945 *City of Manchester Plan: Prepared for the City Council*. Norwich: Jarrold & Sons Ltd

Pevsner, N 1957 'A master plan'. *Hampstead Garden Suburb Jubilee 1907–1957 Souvenir Booklet and Programme* (Hampstead Garden Suburb Archive Trust, S Box 4)

Plinston, H 1981 *A Tale of One City*. Letchworth: Letchworth Garden City Corporation

Purdom, C B 1913 *The Garden City: A Study in the Development of a Modern Town*. London: Dent

Purdom, C B 1925 *The Building of Satellite Towns*. London: Dent

Purdom, C B 1963 *The Letchworth Achievement*. London: Dent

Reid, A 2001 *Brentham. A History of the Pioneer Garden Suburb*. London: Brentham Heritage Society

Saint, A *et al* 1999 *London Suburbs*. London: Merrell Holberton in association with English Heritage

Swenarton, M 1987 *Homes for Heroes*. London: Heinemann Educational Books Ltd

Tarn, J N 1973 *Five Per Cent Philanthropy: An Account of Housing in Urban Areas, 1850–1914*. Cambridge: Cambridge University Press

Town and Country Planning Association 2008 *Policy Advice Note: Garden City Settlements*. *See* http://www.tcpa.org.uk/pages/garden-city-settlements.html (accessed 4 October 2010)

Unwin, R 1909 *Town Planning in Practice*. London: T Fisher Unwin

Unwin, R 1911 *Town Planning in Practice*, 2 edn. London: T Fisher Unwin

Unwin, R 1912 *Nothing Gained by Overcrowding*. London: Garden Cities and Town Planning Association

Gazetteer

A short list of garden city communities in England is given below. Examples can be found in almost every locality: sometimes a few streets or a cul-de-sac, possibly a fragment of a more ambitious scheme that was never fully implemented. Many are already conservation areas. Even when disfigured by later alterations, each will have a history that links it back to the social idealism and design values that were the motivation for building the major examples discussed in this book. Sites are listed by government region and alphabetically within each region.

Abbreviations

BC = Borough Council

CA = Conservation Area

DC = District Council

LB = London Borough

MBC = Metropolitan Borough Council

MCC = Metropolitan City Council

SoM = Scheme of Management

* = World Heritage Site

Authority	Site	Industrial village	Year of foundation	Development notes	Founder	Architect/ planner	CA	SoM
London								
Barking and Dagenham LB	Becontree		1921	Local authority development by London County Council		G Topham Forrest		
Barnet LB: Burnt Oak	Watling Estate		1926	Local authority development by London County Council		G Topham Forrest	Y	
Barnet LB	Hampstead Garden Suburb		1907	Development trust company Co-partnership development	H Barnett	R Unwin B Parker G L Sutcliffe E L Lutyens	Y	Y
Brent LB: Kingsbury	Roe Green Village	A V Roe – aircraft	1916			F Baines	Y	
Croydon: Purley	Webb Estate, Woodcote Village		1888	Developed by W Webb			Y	

Authority	Site	Industrial village	Year of foundation	Development notes	Founder	Architect/ planner	CA	SoM
Ealing LB: Turnham Green	Bedford Park		1875	Developed by J Carr		R N Shaw E J May	Y	
Ealing LB	Brentham Garden Suburb		1901	Co-partnership development with Ealing Tenants		R Unwin F Cavendish Pearson G L Sutcliffe	Y	
Ealing LB: West Acton	GWR Estate	Great Western Railway	1923			T Alwyn Lloyd		
Greenwich LB: Eltham	Well Hall Estate	Ministry of Works –Munitions	1915		F Baines	Y		
Hammersmith and Fulham LB: East Acton	Old Oak Estate		1911	Local authority development by London County Council		W E Riley	Y	
Harringey LB: Muswell Hill	Rookfield Estate		1901	Developed by W J Collins				
Harringey LB: Tottenham	White Hart Lane		1903	Local authority development by London County Council		W E Riley		
Harrow LB: Rayners Lane	Harrow Garden Village		1930	Developed by Metropolitan Railway Country Estates				
Havering LB: Romford	Gidea Park Garden Suburb		1910/1934	Developed by Gidea Park Ltd			Y	

Authority	Site	Industrial village	Year of foundation	Development notes	Founder	Architect/ planner	CA	SoM
Hillingdon LB	Manor Way		1911	Development Company Co-partnership development		A and J Soutar	Y	
Hillingdon LB	Ruislip Manor		1930s	Development Company Co-partnership development		A and J Soutar		
Lewisham LB	Bellingham Estate		1921	Local authority development by London County Council		G Topham Forrest		
Sutton LB	Sutton Garden Suburb		1912	Development company Co-partnership development		F Cavendish Pearson		
Wandsworth LB: Tooting	Totterdown Fields Estate		1901	Local authority development by London County Council		W E Riley	Y	

South-East

Authority	Site	Industrial village	Year of foundation	Development notes	Founder	Architect/ planner	CA	SoM
Buckinghamshire: Chiltern DC	Jordans Village		1919	Developed by the Society of Friends		F Rowntree	Y	
Hertfordshire	Letchworth Garden City		1903	Development company Co-partnership development		Parker and Unwin Bennett and Bidwell C M Crickmer		

Authority	Site	Industrial village	Year of foundation	Development notes	Founder	Architect/ planner	CA	SoM
Milton Keynes BC	Wolverton	London and Birmingham Railway	1840				Y	
Surrey: Elmbridge DC	Cobham Whiteley Village – retirement village		1911	Developed by the estate trust of W Whiteley		F Atkinson R Blomfield A Webb E Newton	Y	
Welwyn Hatfield BC	Welwyn Garden City – new town		1920	Development company and local authority development	E Howard	Louis de Soissons	Y	Y
Winchester City	Stanmore Estate		1920	Local authority development		W Dunn W Curtis Green		

South-West

Bristol City	Sea Mills Estate		1919	Local authority development		C F W Dening	Y	
Swindon BC	Swindon Railway Village	Great Western Railway	1840s				Y	

East of England

Bedford BC	Shortstown	Short Bros – later RAF	1917					
Bedford BC	Stewartby	London Brick Co	1927			E Vincent Harris		
Braintree DC	Silver End	F H Crittall & Co – windows	1926			C M Hennell T Tait F MacManus	Y	

Authority	Site	Industrial village	Year of foundation	Development notes	Founder	Architect/ planner	CA	SoM
Thurrock BC	East Tilbury, Bata Estate	Bata Shoe Co	1933			F Gahura V Karfik	Y	
North Herts DC	Knebworth Garden Village		1908	Development company Co-partnership development with Knebworth Tenants	Lord Lytton	T Adams E L Lutyens Pepler and Allen	Y	

East Midlands

Authority	Site	Industrial village	Year of foundation	Development notes	Founder	Architect/ planner	CA	SoM
Derbyshire: Bolsover DC	Cresswell Model Village	Bolsover and Cresswell Colliery	1896				Y	
Derbyshire: Bolsover DC	New Bolsover	Bolsover and Cresswell Colliery	1888				Y	
Leicestershire: Charnwood BC, Loughborough	Shelthorpe Estate		1925			B Parker	Y	
Leicestershire: Charnwood BC	Rothley Ridgeway		1909	Developed by Frederick Merttens			Y	
Leicester City	Humberstone Garden Village	Anchor Boot and Shoe Co-op	1906	Co-partnership development with Anchor Tenants		R Unwin		
Lincoln City	Swanpool Garden Suburb		1919	Developed by a public utility organisation		A Thompson C M Hennell C H James		

Authority	Site	Industrial village	Year of foundation	Development notes	Founder	Architect/ planner	CA	SoM
West Midlands								
Birmingham	Bournville	Cadbury – chocolate	1895	Developed by the Bourneville Village Trust	G Cadbury	W A Harvey H Bedford Tylor	Y	Y
Birmingham	Harborne, Moor Pool		1908	Co-partnership development with Harborne Tenants		Martin and Martin	Y	
Birmingham City	Perry Barr, Kingstanding		1928	Local authority development				
Wolverhampton City	Fallings Park		1908	Development Company Co-partnership development with Garden City Tenants		D Blow T Adams		
Yorkshire and the Humber								
Bradford MCC	Saltaire	Sir Titus Salt – textile mills	1851			Lockwood and Mawson	Y*	
Calderdale MBC	Akroydon	Edward Akroyd – textile mills	1861			G Scott W H Crosland	Y	
Doncaster MBC	New Rossington Village	Rossington Main Colliery, Industrial Housing Association Ltd	1920s	Developed by Sir J Tudor Walters and Lord Aberconway		B Parker		
Doncaster MBC	Woodlands Village	Brodsworth Main Colliery	1908			P Houfton		
Hull City	Hull Garden Village	Sir James Reckitt	1907			P T Runton W E Barry	Y	

Authority	Site	Industrial village	Year of foundation	Development notes	Founder	Architect/ planner	CA	SoM
York City	New Earswick	J Rowntree – chocolate	1902			Parker and Unwin B Parker	Y	

North-West

Authority	Site	Industrial village	Year of foundation	Development notes	Founder	Architect/ planner	CA	SoM
Cumbria: Barrow-in-Furness BC	Vickerstown	Vickers Shipbuilding	1898				Y	
Manchester City	Burnage Garden Village		1906	Co-partnership development with Manchester Tenants		J Horner Hargreaves		
Manchester City	Wythenshawe		1931	Local authority development		B Parker R Nicholas		
Merseyside: Liverpool City	Speke Estate		1936	Local authority development		Sir Lancelot Keay		
Merseyside: Liverpool City	Wavetree Garden Suburb		1910	Co-partnership development		R Unwin G L Sutcliffe	Y	
Merseyside: Wirral MBC	Bromborough Pool	Prices Patent Candle Co	1853			J Hill	Y	
Merseyside: Wirral MBC	Port Sunlight	Lever Bros Soap	1888			W and S Owen Douglas and Fordham	Y	Y
Merseyside: Wirral MB	Thornton Hough		1867	Developed by J Hirst (1867–71) and W H Lever (1892–1907)		Kirk and Sons (J Hirst) W and S Owen Douglas and Fordham (W H Lever)	Y	

North-East

Authority	Site	Industrial village	Year of foundation	Development notes	Founder	Architect/ planner	CA	SoM
Redcar and Cleveland BC	Dormanstown	Dorman Long – steelfounders	1918			Adshead and Ramsay P Abercrombie		

Other titles in the Informed Conservation series

Alston Moor: Buildings in a North Pennines landscape.
Lucy Jessop and Matthew Whitfield, with Andrew Davison, 2013.
Product code 51755, ISBN 9781848021174

Ancoats: Cradle of industrialisation.
Michael E Rose with Keith Falconer and Julian Holder, 2011.
Product code 51453, ISBN 9781848020276

Berwick-upon-Tweed: Three places, two nations, one town.
Adam Menuge with Catherine Dewar, 2009.
Product code 51471, ISBN 9781848020290

Building a Better Society: Liverpool's historic institutional buildings.
Colum Giles, 2008.
Product code 51332, ISBN 9781873592908

Built on Commerce: Liverpool's central business district.
Joseph Sharples and John Stonard, 2008.
Product code 51331, ISBN 9781905624348

Defending Scilly.
Mark Bowden and Allan Brodie, 2011.
Product code 51530, ISBN 9781848020436

England's Schools: History, architecture and adaptation.
Elain Harwood, 2010.
Product code 51476, ISBN 9781848020313

English Garden Cities: An introduction.
Mervyn Miller, 2010.
Product code 51532, ISBN 9781848020511

The Hat Industry of Luton and its Buildings.
Katie Carmichael, David McOmish and David Grech, 2013.
Product code 51750, ISBN 9781848021198

Manchester's Northern Quarter.
Simon Taylor and Julian Holder, 2008.
Product code 50946, ISBN 9781873592847

Manchester: The warehouse legacy – An introduction and guide.
Simon Taylor, Malcolm Cooper and P S Barnwell, 2002.
Product code 50668, ISBN 9781873592670

Manningham: Character and diversity in a Bradford suburb
Simon Taylor and Kathryn Gibson, 2010.
Product code 51475, ISBN 9781848020306

Margate's Seaside Heritage.
Nigel Barker, Allan Brodie, Nick Dermott, Lucy Jessop
and Gary Winter, 2007.
Product code 51335, ISBN 9781905624669

Ordinary Landscapes, Special Places: Anfield, Breckfield and the growth of Liverpool's suburbs.
Adam Menuge, 2008.
Product code 51343, ISBN 9781873592892

Places of Health and Amusement: Liverpool's historic parks and gardens.
Katy Layton-Jones and Robert Lee, 2008.
Product code 51333, ISBN 9781873592915

Religion and Place in Leeds.
John Minnis with Trevor Mitchell, 2007.
Product code 51337, ISBN 9781905624485

Stourport-on-Severn: Pioneer town of the canal age.
Colum Giles, Keith Falconer, Barry Jones and Michael Taylor, 2007.
Product code 51290, ISBN 9781905624362

Weymouth's Seaside Heritage.
Allan Brodie, Colin Ellis, David Stuart and Gary Winter, 2008.
Product code 51429, ISBN 9781848020085

Further information on titles in the Informed Conservation series can be found on our website.

To order through EH Sales
Tel: 01235 465577
Fax: 01235 465556
Email: direct.orders@marston.co.uk

Online bookshop: www.english-heritageshop.org.uk